BAND...
YOU CALL IT?

If you love this
Coke or Pepsi?
book, then check
out more

books for you & your friends.

Coke or Pepsi?

More Coke or Pepsi?

Coke or Pepsi? 3

My Best Year
Fill in the blanks of your life.

coke-or-pepsi.com

the Ultimate coke OR pepsi?

What do you really know about your friends?

FINE print
PUBLISHING

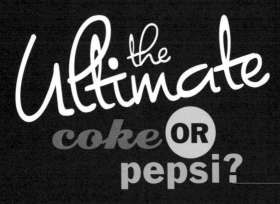

the Ultimate coke OR pepsi?

Written and designed by
Mickey & Cheryl Gill

Fine Print Publishing Company
P.O. Box 916401
Longwood, Florida 32971-6401

Created in the U.S.A. & Printed in China
This book is printed on acid-free paper

ISBN 978-1-892951-44-1

10 9 8 7 6 5 4

coke-or-pepsi.com

Pass this book around to all of your friends. Each friend has a chance to answer some pretty cool questions.

See what you have in common. Find out what makes you different. Some answers might even shock you!

Answer a set of questions & pass it back.

WHAT'S MOST FUN TO POP? ● POPCORN ◉ BUBBLE WRAP ● BALLOONS?

SOMETHING U OWN THAT WOULD SURPRISE FRIENDS?

JEANS W/ ● FLIP-FLOPS ● FLATS ● HEELS ● SNEAKERS?

MOVIE CHARACTER U'D LIKE TO BE?

stick a
pic of →
you here

Property of ___Redyun___
name

5ive RANDOM things about me

1. My fave junk food/soft drink combo is _____

2. i know how to _____
something u r good at

and _____ but not at the same time.
something u r good at

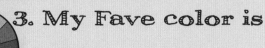

3. My Fave color is

_____

4. 1 LUV 2 WEAR _____

5. The coolest thing I've ever done is

_____

pick me

pick me

pick me

If you were a dog, what kind would u be?

NAME _____

1. If u were a dog, what kind would u be?_____

2. Choose a secret agent name 4 yourself – _____

3. **Which is worth it?** ○ mouth on FIRE from hot sauce ◉ ice cream brain freeze ○ neither!

4. **EAT M&M'S** ® ○ 1 @ A time ○ BY the HANDFUL?

5. Ever made a snow angel? ◉ YEP ○ NOPE ○ WHAT IS THAT?!

6. **ULTIMATE part of a cake?** ○ cake ○ frosting ○ filling

7. ○ Dancing ○ Listening to music?

8. Ever complete a puzzle? ◉ YES ○ NO, HOW BORING!

9. What sweet food could u never, ever give up? yum lolly pop sour keys

10. I wish I could be paid to ~~brownies~~ eat a smothing mashashchir

11. HOW MANY TEETH DO U HAVE? _____

12. How many fillings do u have? _____

13. Do toothpaste WORMS in the sink bug u? ◉ YES! ○ NO ○ WHAT?!

14. **Ever been sent to the principal's office?** ◉ NO ○ YES, what 4? _____

15. Is it worth being sick to miss school? ○ YEP ○ NOPE ◉ SOMETIMES

16. When do u make your bed? ○ a.m. ◉ when I'm told 2 ○ uh, never?

17. ○ Untie ○ Kick off sneakers?

18. Ever take the blame 4 something someone else did? ○ YES ◉ NO

19. Ever blamed someone else 4 something u did? ○ YES :(○ NO

20. **Magical power u wish u had?** TO FLY

don't even think about it

NAME _____

1. Would u rather be a ○ cat & wash yourself ● dog & get a bath?

2. Something guys **LUV** that u just don't get? _tu fart and burp_

3. ULTIMATE **WINTER** Olympic sport? _Skiing_

4. ULTIMATE *summer* Olympic sport? _____

5. Ever wear socks with holes in them? ● Sure, if they don't show ○ NO!

6. I would **LUV** to take care of a ○ baby ● puppy ○ kitten.

7. Star ○ gazing (as in the sky) ○ watching (as in Hollywood)?

8. Open your mouth to put on mascara? ○ YEAH, WEIRD ○ NO ○ DON'T WEAR IT

9. What's ur earliest memory? _____

10. Ever fed a goat? ● of course ○ nah ○ ew, no, don't they eat your clothes?

11. COOLEST thing you've ever made by hand? _____

12. Singer whose songs u own the most of? _____

13. Spit out yucky food & ● hide in napkin ○ put back on plate?

14. Afraid of public speaking? ○ absolutely ● kind of ○ nope

15. ○ Grapes ○ Raisins ○ Neither?

16. What's under your bed? _____

17. **EVER BEEN** HYPNOTiZED? ○ YES ● NO

18. Habit you'd want to break with hypnosis? _____

19. Concert you'd like a backstage pass 4? _____

20. **Celebrity crush u have?** _____

I wish mermaids were real

NAME _____

1. Something make-believe that u wish was real? _Unicorn_____

2. Something real that u wish was make-believe? _____

3. Last conversation I had was with _____ about _____.

4. Where do u do most of your heavy thinking? _In my room_____

5. Wash hair ○ every day ○ every other day ○ twice a week?

6. **ULTIMATE ROAD TRIP GAME?** _____

7. ○ **Patient** ○ **Impatient?**

8. Something u own that would surprise friends? _____

9. ○ Early ○ On time ○ Late person?

10. **SOMETHING DUMB U DID AS A LITTLE KID?** _____

11. Ever used a toothpick? ● *yes, don't tell anyone* ○ *no way*

12. How do u wear your hair most of the time? _down_____

13. Ever gotten into poison ivy? ○ *yes! itchy!* ○ *no*

14. Ever dress up your pet? ○ no pet :(○ no! ● yes! With what? _____

15. **Talk during movies?** ○ **never** ● **sometimes a little** ○ **always**

16. Sing in the shower? ● *no* ○ *yes. How do u sound?* _____

17. Scared of clowns? ○ *oh yeah* ● *nah*

18. ○ First ○ Last to raise your hand in class?

19. ○ Stick to plans ○ Wing it?

20. R u a ○ good ○ great ○ awful photographer?

Guitar Hero® of course

NAME _____

1. **ULTIMATE** video game? _Tel/pell vun_

2. Ever been seriously lost? ● no ○ yes ↘
   What happened? _____

3. Friend ur similar 2? _Emma_

4. Friend ur the exact opposite of? _____

5. How many pairs of jeans do u own? _____

6. Ever written a poem? ● *No way* ○ yes

7. ○ Mexican ○ Chinese ○ Pizza?

8. Iron your clothes in the a.m.? ○ of course ● r u kidding?

9. Know anyone u think can read ur mind? ● *no* ○ yes ↘
   Who? _____

10. ○ Chocolate mints ○ Mint gum ○ Hard mint candies?

11. Your house is on fire!
    ↘ *What 1 item would u save?* _____

12. ○ Black
    ○ Refried beans?

13. ○ Cookies ○ Candy?

14. ○ Secret garden ○ Public park?

15. Own slippers? ○ *no* ○ yes ↘
    What do they look like? _____

16. R u most like ○ SpongeBob ● Patrick ○ Squidward?

17. Most nutritious food u actually like to eat? _____

18. If u could only wear 1 outfit for 1 year
    ↘ *what would it be?* _____

19. Caught not paying attention in class? ● no ○ of course!

20. Ever been grounded?
○ no ○ yes.
What 4? _____

Star-Struck

Name_____

I would **LUV** to star opposite _____ actor _____ *in a movie.*

It would be so **Cool** to co-star with _____ actress _____ *in a movie.*

Fave movie character? _____

SCARIEST MOVIE MONSTER? _____

WORST MOVIE U'VE SEEN THIS YEAR? _____

GRAND

BEST MOVIE U'VE SEEN THIS YEAR?

2 FAVE FLICK?

OK, # 3?

Y is it your Fave?

Hottest actor?

Hottest actress?

Best movie kiss?

Fave way to see a flick?
○ big screen TV at home
○ stadium seating theater
⦿ small local theater

Best seat in the theater?
⦿ up high, in the back
○ middle
○ front & center

POPCORN
(check all that apply)
⦿ S ○ M ○ L ○ plain ○ butter ⦿ xtra butter

Best theater food? all of it

*If u were an actor,
what's the 1st thing u would buy when u made it big?*

Where would u live? ⦿ NYC ○ LA ○ other

Like
black & white
movies?
○ yes ○ no

Ever watch
a film w/
subtitles?
○ oui ○ no

Watch
the
Oscars?
○ yes ○ no

Best
chick
flick?
_____

If I had a band,

1. **IF YOU HAD A BAND, WHAT WOULD U CALL IT?** Name _girls rowk_

2. What's most fun to pop? ○ popcorn ● bubble wrap ○ balloons?

3. What's your screensaver? _____

4. Jeans with ○ flip-flops ○ flats ○ heels ○ sneakers?

5. *I luv the sound of* _____.

6. Do straw slurping sounds bug u? ○ yes ○ no

7. How 'bout nails on a chalkboard? ○ yes ○ no

8. Hottest place u've ever been? _____

9. Coldest place u've ever been? _____

10. Do u have ○ awful ○ OK ○ great handwriting?

11. **ULTIMATE romantic movie?** _____

12. Who do you usually see movies with? _____

13. ○ Candlelight ○ Lamplight ○ Flashlight?

14. What do ur sunglasses look like? _____

15. ○ **Country house** ○ Big city condo

16. Coolest person u know? _____

17. Most stylish person u know? _____

18. Funniest person u know? _____

19. Most annoying? ○ bad breath ○ smacking gum ○ talking with mouth full

20. Something u say ur going 2 do but never do? _____

I would name it after me.

Name Deaiah

1. SOMETHING U'D LUV TO WEAR BUT DON'T HAVE THE NERVE? _____

2. Scared 2 travel over tall bridges? ○ oh yeah ● no way, it's safe

3. Ever had food poisoning? ○ no ● yes. What did u eat? _big clam bar_

4. Had an ant farm? ○ yes ○ no ○ just the idea makes me sting!

5. Grown Sea-Monkeys®? ○ oh yeah ○ no ○ what r those?

6. Who do u text the most? _____

7. Rescued a wild animal? ○ no ○ yes. What kind? _____

8. R u ticklish? ○ YES! AHH! ○ not really

9. ○ From scratch ○ from a box ○ no mac & cheese?

10. I wish my family had a _____

11. Which is worst? ○ Gnats ○ Flies ○ Mosquitoes?

12. Watch TV while u eat dinner? ○ always ○ sometimes ○ never

13. *Magazine cover u would like to appear on?* _____

14. ○ Fall asleep in ○ Scared to death of the dentist's chair?

15. Take the road ○ less travelled ○ everyone else follows?

16. Any nervous habits? ○ nope ○ yes. What? _____

17. Can u do a backbend? ○ yep ○ no, ow!

18. ULTIMATE sundae ingredients? _____

19. Can u tie a knot in a cherry stem with your tongue? ○ no ○ yep ○ huh?

20. What could u write a book about? _____

my tunes

Name _____

What r your top 3 fave bands?
1.
2.
3.

What r your top five fave songs?

Title
_____

_____ is perfect to dance to.

Title
_____

_____ is great to sing with.

Title
_____

_____ has the coolest lyrics.

Title
_____

_____ has awesome music.

Title
_____

_____ is the best overall song.

What's on ur playlist?
(check all that apply)
- rock
- pop
- alternative
- country
- dance
- rap/hip hop
- other _____

CONCERT IN A
⬤ BIG STADIUM ⬤ COOL DANCE CLUB ⬤ SMALL, INTIMATE CLUB?

SEEN ANYONE IN CONCERT? ⬤ NOPE ⬤ YEP. WHO?
_____

WHO R U DYING TO SEE IN CONCERT?
_____

my tunes

Coolest male singer?
_____

Hottest female singer?
_____

Best performer look?
- ○ JEANS & A T-SHIRT
- ○ SUPER GLAM
- ○ ANYTHING + A COWBOY HAT

dance

- ○ with friends
- ○ alone in your house?
  (in front of a mirror?)
  - ○ of course
  - ○ no way!

Coolest lyrics
from a song?

Lyrics _____

_____

_____

_____

_____

Song Title

OH

LAST
ALBUM U
BOUGHT?
_____
_____

○ I don't buy ENTIRE Albums! I NEVER like ALL the songs.

COLOR IN THE LINES?

Name **Reagan 2014**

1. color in the lines? ○ no ● yes

2. How many pillows do you sleep with? **One**

3. ● Team ○ Individual sports?

4. Can u read music? ○ yes ● no

5. What's worth waking up really early 4? **Soccer games**

6. Believe in haunted houses? ○ yes, scary! ● no, it's all a hoax!

7. How about psychics? ○ yes ● no, it's a scam

8. Swim in ● a pool (boring?) ○ a lake (alligators?) ○ the ocean (sharks?)

9. If u could only have 1 hobby, what would it be? **Sports**

10. Libraries r ○ so cool ○ too quiet ● OK, I guess

11. IF WE HAD 2 B NAMED AFTER PLANETS, WHICH WOULD U CHOOSE? **Saturn**

12. How about a city? **New York**

13. WHAT ABOUT A COLOR? **Violet**

14. Chew on ice? ○ no way, that's bad 4 u ● oh yeah

15. Bird ever drop something (u know!) on u? ○ yes, gross! ● nope

16. Eakspa igpa atinla? ● WHAT?! ○ esya, Ia oda

17. ULTIMATE fried food? **french fries**

18. Fave color to write with? ○ black ○ blue ● other **Violet**

19. Send ● really wordy ○ super short text messages?

20. Ever drunk wheat grass? ● no ○ yes

How was it? _____

HOW BORING!

nice

Name _____

1. Color things the correct colors (GREEN GRASS, BLUE SKY)? ○ **yes** ○ **no,** how boring!

2. ○ Cityscape ○ Ocean sunset ○ Mountain view?

3. Won an award? ○ **nah** ○ **yes.** What 4? _____

4. ○ Sweet ○ Sour ○ Sweet & Sour?

5. ○ **Store-bought** ○ **Homemade Valentine?**

6. Best food when it's cold outside? _____

7. How about when it's hot? _____

8. ○ Big ○ Medium ○ Little dogs?

9. ○ **BLUSH** ○ **BUBBLEGUM** ○ **HOT** ○ **NO PINK?**

10. *Meanest* thing a sibling's done 2 u? _____

11. *Nicest* thing a sibling's done 4 u? _____

12. Sit ○ up front ○ in the middle ○ in the back of class?

13. **I could beat** _____ **in an arm wrestling match.**

14. Ridden on a horse? ○ **yes** ○ **no**

15. **ULTIMATE TV network?** _____

16. Keep a diary? ○ **no** ○ **yes**

17. Read someone else's diary? ○ **no,** that's private! ○ **yeah,** I feel bad.

18. New Year's resolutions? ○ **no** ○ **yes.** This year's? _____

19. **MET A CELEBRITY?** ○ **no** ○ **yes,** Who? _____

20. How's your singing? ○ Awful! ○ OK ○ Better than average ○ Awesome!

DESERT ISLAND

YOU ARE stranded on a remote island for 1 year...
make wise choices OR if u really want to laugh,
write down the 1st thing that comes to ur mind.

U can have one food item (besides ALL the fish you can catch!)
What would u choose?

> cheeseburger

1 BEVERAGE? (Besides fresh H2O)

> Sprite

What ONE outfit would U
bring to wear?

Top _cape cod sweat_
shirt and I ♡ beach
Bottom _bikini bottom_
and strechy jeans
Shoes _tennis shoes_

1 AUTHOR
You get all the books they've ever written.

> J.K. Rowling

1 MAGAZINE ➡
Don't worry, you'll get one a month!

> American Girl

1 FREEBIE ITEM — IT CAN BE ANYTHING . . .

but ur cell phone, most likely won't have good reception . . .
so think of something else.

lighter

While struggling to survive, what cool thing could u do for 1 whole year?

climb mountains

BEST THING ABOUT SOLO ISLAND LIVING?

- the beach
- ✓ do WHATEVER I want
- great tan
- lots of "alone" time

ICKIEST THING ABOUT UR SO-CALLED PARADISE?

- ✓ too much alone time
- awful sunburn
- learning to fish
- SAND!! in everything!

U R FINALLY RESCUED!

YAY!

1st person u'd want to see?

Mom+ Dad

1st thing u'd want to do? ➜ Sleep in bed

1st thing u'd want to eat? ➜ Spaghetti

HELP!

Do U stare @ people?

Name_____

1. **Do U** stare @ people? ◯ No, how rude! ◯ Depends ◯ Of course, I can't help it

2. Something u like. (1ST THING THAT COMES TO MiND): _____

3. Something u dislike. (1ST THING THAT COMES TO MiND): _____

4. **Strawberry** ◯ **shortcake** ◯ **milkshake** ◯ **jam?**

5. IF U WERE FAMOUS, WHAT WOULD BE UR STAGE NAME? _____

6. Do u like hugging? ◯ yes ◯ not really, it invades my personal space

7. WHAT SPORT DO U REALLY STINK @?_____

8. Ever take ballet? ◯ **yes** ◯ **no**

9. Watch sports on TV ? ◯ **no way** ◯ **yes.** What? _____

10. Make any cool sound effects? ◯ **nah** ◯ **yes.** What? _____

11. R u good at imitating people? ◯ **no** ◯ **sort of** ◯ **yes**

12. Name of fave stuffed animal when u were a kid? _____

13. FUNNiEST aCTOR? _____

14. Stuck a piece of chewed gum somewhere? ◯ **no, yuck!** ◯ **yes.** _____
↖where?

15. **ULTIMATE** CURE 4 hiccups? _____

16. **What's most important to u?** ◯ looks ◯ smarts ◯ popularity ◯ other_____

17. Ugliest shoes u've owned? _____

18. Spilled something on urself in public? ◯ **no** ◯ **yes.** What? _____

19. Spilled something on someone else? ◯ **no** ◯ **yes.** What? _____

20. Have a crush on someone? ◯ **not right now** ◯ **yeah**

What do U think?

Name _____

1. PERFORMED IN FRONT OF AN AUDIENCE? ◯ NO ◯ YES. WHAT 4? _____

2. **ULTIMATE** condiment? ◯ Mayo ◯ Mustard ◯ Ketchup ◯ All, mixed together

3. What mall store defines your personality? _____

4. 1 thing u argue about w/ parents? _____

5. Fold your underwear? ◯ **yes** ◯ **r u joking?**

6. ◯ It's hard ◯ I don't like ◯ I LUV to make new friends?

7. Something ur family does together that u LUV? _____

8. Something ur family does together that u can't stand? _____

9. **HELD A BABY CHICK?** ◯ **yep** ◯ **nope**

10. Been in a parade? ◯ **no** ◯ **yes.** What didja do? _____

11. Good @ solving mysteries in movies? ◯ **no** ◯ **yes,** I should be a detective!

12. **R U A FREAKY CHANNEL SURFER?** ◯ **oh yeah** ◯ **no,** *that's SO ANNOYING!*

13. Most creative thing u've done? _____

14. WOULD U GIVE SOMEONE A PEDICURE? ◯ **no,** FEET R GROSS! ◯ **sure.**

15. Jealous of a brother/sister? ◯ **no** ◯ **yes.** Y? _____

16. Do u brag? ◯ **no** ◯ **sure** ◯ **ugh, I think so**

17. Speak another language? ◯ **nope** ◯ **yes.** What? _____

18. WOULD U RATHER ◯ GLOW IN THE DARK ◯ SHIMMER IN THE DAYLIGHT?

19. Left an awful movie? ◯ **nah** ◯ **yes.** Name? _____

20. My 1st crush was _____ when I was _____ yrs. old.

1. SKELETONS ◯ GIVE ME THE CREEPS! EW! ◯ R SO COOL!

2. Fave game show? _____

3. Game show u think u MIGHT do well on?_____

4. ◯ Strawberries ◯ Bananas ◯ Oranges ◯ Apples
   ◯ Pears ◯ Other _____ ?

NAME _____

5. Ever picked your own fruit/veggies from a farm?
   ◯ NO ◯ YES. What? _____

6. ◯ Piano ◯ Acoustic guitar ◯ Electric guitar
   ◯ Saxophone ◯ Other _____?

7. I ◯ can't stand being too busy
   ◯ LUV having too much going on.

8. Embarrassing celebrity crush u had when you
   were younger? _____

9. Ever gone to camp? ◯ NO ◯ YES
   Name of it? _____

10. Want to be in politics?
    ◯ Yeah, it would B really cool ◯ R u kidding me?!

11. I stink at anything requiring ◯ artistic ◯ scientific skills.

12. ◯ Klutzy ◯ Perfectly coordinated?

13. ULTIMATE movie soundtrack? _____

14. Something u bought that u regret? _____

15. Grossest thing boys do? _____

16. I escape by ◯ listening to music ◯ watching TV
    ◯ getting lost in a book ◯ taking a nap.

17. SCARED 2 STAY ALONE IN UR HOUSE @ NIGHT? ◯ ALWAYS ◯ SOMETIMES ◯ NOPE

18. Celebrity U would love 2 interview? _____

19. Nickname? ◯ NO ◯ YES. How'd u get it?
    _____

20. R U named after anyone? ◯ NO ◯ YES. Who?_____

1. Which is scariest? ⚪ **VAMPIRE** ☑ **ZOMBIE** ⚪ WITCH ⚪ None, they're not real!

2. Last thing u watched on YouTube? _Corl_

3. Ever been on YouTube? ⚪ **NO** ☑ **YES**

4. Wish u had a twin? ⚪ no way! ☑ yeah, that would b cool.

5. If ur BFF were a food, what would she/he be?
   Strawbery

6. Cops ☑ make me feel safe ⚪ kinda scare me.

7. Seen a waterfall? ⚪ **NO** ☑ **YES.** Which one(s)?
   Niagra Falls

8. ⚪ **MySpace** ⚪ **Facebook** ☑ **other** _Musicly_ ?

9. I would LUV to be famous 4 _Olympics_
   _____.

10. If u had wings, where would u fly 2?
    _____ Y? _____

11. If ur personality were a car, what would it be?
    _____

12. READ UR HOROSCOPE? ⚪ YES, FOR FUN ⚪ NO, IT'S ALL MADE UP

13. **ULTIMATE adventure w/ a friend?** _____
    _____

14. I mostly like to be around
    ⚪ funny ⚪ smart ⚪ warm-hearted people.

15. Make wishes & throw coins into fountains? ⚪ **YES** ⚪ **NAH**

16. I ⚪ like to please people ⚪ don't care what others think.

17. Eat sushi? ⚪ **NO, GROSS!** ⚪ **YES.** Fave kind? _____
    _____

18. It's cooler to hang out with ⚪ girls ⚪ guys.

19. Something u believed as a little kid? _____

20. I think most people think I'm ⚪ funny ⚪ snobby ⚪ friendly ⚪ weird.

Name _____

style
conscious

I luv to shop for my clothes @
1. _____
2. _____
3. _____

Store u like 2 visit but usually don't buy from?

_____

Last accessory u bought?

_____

Do u own something
you've never worn?
⬤ No ⬤ Yes
What? _____

I

⬤ put a lot of thought
into what I wear.

⬤ throw my clothes on
quickly.

⬤ just like to be
comfortable.

If I could, I would wear _____ every day.

my closet is mostly full of

⬤ jeans ⬤ skirts ⬤ tops ⬤ other _____.

Most comfortable article of clothing I own is my

_____.

What hat would u never, ever wear?
- baseball cap
- cowboy hat
- beret
- other _____
- I would try any of them. I LUV hats!

What's ur style?

- preppy – smart, not opposed to plaid
- boho – romantic, billowy, artsy
- punk – edgy, crazy, rock 'n' roll
- diva – all glam, glitzy, probably like pink
- I don't fit into these molds! Then describe your style. ↘

_____
_____
_____
_____
_____
_____
_____

my faves

T-shirt	Shoes
Dress	Bag
Sweater	Earrings

pick me

pick me

pick me

If you were a dog, what kind would u be?

NAME _____

1. If u were a dog, what kind would u be? _____

2. Choose a secret agent name 4 yourself – _____

3. **Which is worth it?** ○ mouth on FIRE from hot sauce ○ ice cream brain freeze ○ neither!

4. eAt M&M'S ® ○ 1 @ A tIme ○ BY the HANDFUL?

5. Ever made a snow angel? ○ YEp ○ NOPE ○ WHAT IS THAT?!

6. ULTIMATE **part of a cake?** ○ cake ○ frosting ○ filling

7. ○ Dancing ○ Listening to music?

8. Ever complete a puzzle? ○ YES ○ NO, HOW BORING!

9. What sweet food could u never, ever give up? _____

10. I wish I could be paid to _____.

11. HOW MANY TEETH do U HaVe? _____

12. How many fillings do u have? _____

13. Do toothpaste WoRMS in the sink bug u? ○ YES! ○ NO ○ WHAT?!

14. **Ever been sent to the principal's office?** ○ NO ○ YES, what 4? _____

15. Is it worth being sick to miss school? ○ YEp ○ NOPE ○ SOMETIMES

16. When do u make your bed? ○ a.m. ○ when I'm told 2 ○ uh, never?

17. ○ Untie ○ Kick off sneakers?

18. Ever take the blame 4 something someone else did? ○ YES ○ NO

19. Ever blamed someone else 4 something u did? ○ YES :(○ NO

20. Magical power u wish u had? _____

don't even think about it

NAME _____

1. Would u rather be a ⃝ cat & wash yourself ⃝ dog & get a bath?

2. Something guys **LUV** that u just don't get? _____

3. ULTIMATE **WINTER** Olympic sport? _____

4. ULTIMATE *summer* Olympic sport? _____

5. Ever wear socks with holes in them? ⃝ Sure, if they don't show ⃝ NO!

6. I would **LUV** to take care of a ⃝ baby ⃝ puppy ⃝ kitten.

7. Star ⃝ gazing (as in the sky) ⃝ watching (as in Hollywood)?

8. Open your mouth to put on mascara? ⃝ YEAH, WEIRD ⃝ NO ⃝ DON'T WEAR IT

9. What's ur earliest memory? _____

10. Ever fed a goat? ⃝ of course ⃝ nah ⃝ ew, no, don't they eat your clothes?

11. **COOLEST** thing you've ever made by hand? _____

12. Singer whose songs u own the most of? _____

13. Spit out yucky food & ⃝ hide in napkin ⃝ put back on plate?

14. Afraid of public speaking? ⃝ absolutely ⃝ kind of ⃝ nope

15. ⃝ Grapes ⃝ Raisins ⃝ Neither?

16. What's under your bed? _____

17. **EVER BEEN HYPNOTIZED?** ⃝ YES ⃝ NO

18. Habit you'd want to break with hypnosis? _____

19. Concert you'd like a backstage pass 4? _____

20. **Celebrity crush u have?** _____

I wish mermaids were real

NAME _____

1. Something make-believe that u wish was real? _____

2. Something real that u wish was make-believe? _____

3. Last conversation I had was with _____ about _____.

4. Where do u do most of your heavy thinking? _____

5. Wash hair ◯ every day ◯ every other day ◯ twice a week?

6. ULTIMATE ROAD TRIP GAME? _____

7. ◯ Patient ◯ Impatient?

8. Something u own that would surprise friends? _____

9. ◯ Early ◯ On time ◯ Late person?

10. SOMETHING DUMB U DID as a LiTTLE KiD? _____

11. Ever used a toothpick? ◯ yes, don't tell anyone ◯ No way

12. How do u wear your hair most of the time? _____

13. Ever gotten into poison ivy? ◯ yes! itchy! ◯ No

14. Ever dress up your pet? ◯ no pet :(◯ no! ◯ yes! With what? _____

15. **Talk during movies?** ◯ never ◯ sometimes a little ◯ always

16. Sing in the shower? ◯ No ◯ yes. How do u sound? _____

17. Scared of clowns? ◯ oh yeah ◯ nah

18. ◯ First ◯ Last to raise your hand in class?

19. ◯ Stick to plans ◯ Wing it?

20. R u a ◯ good ◯ great ◯ awful photographer?

Guitar Hero® of course

NAME _____

1. ULTIMATE video game? _____

2. Ever been seriously lost? ◯ no ◯ yes ↘
   What happened? _____

3. Friend ur similar 2? _____

4. Friend ur the exact opposite of? _____

5. How many pairs of jeans do u own? _____

6. Ever written a poem? ◯ *No way* ◯ *yes*

7. ◯ Mexican ◯ Chinese ◯ Pizza?

8. Iron your clothes in the a.m.? ◯ of course ◯ r u kidding?

9. Know anyone u think can read ur mind? ◯ *No* ◯ *yes* ↘
   Who? _____

10. ◯ Chocolate mints ◯ Mint gum ◯ Hard mint candies?

11. Your house is on fire!
    ↳ *What 1 item would u save?* _____

12. ◯ Black
    ◯ Refried beans?

13. ◯ Cookies ◯ Candy?

14. ◯ Secret garden ◯ Public park?

15. Own slippers? ◯ *No* ◯ *yes* ↘
    What do they look like? _____

16. R u most like ◯ SpongeBob ◯ Patrick ◯ Squidward?

17. Most nutritious food u actually like to eat? _____

18. If u could only wear 1 outfit for 1 year
    ↳ *what would it be?* _____

20. Ever been grounded?
◯ no ◯ yes.
What 4? _____
_____

19. Caught not paying attention in class? ◯ no ◯ of course!

Star-Struck

Name_____

I would **LUV** to star opposite _____ in a movie.
actor

It would be so **Cool** to co-star with _____ in a movie.
actress

Fave movie character?

SCARIEST MOVIE MONSTER?

WORST MOVIE U'VE SEEN THIS YEAR?

GRAND

BEST MOVIE U'VE SEEN THIS YEAR?

2 FAVE FLICK?

OK, # 3?

Y is it your Fave?

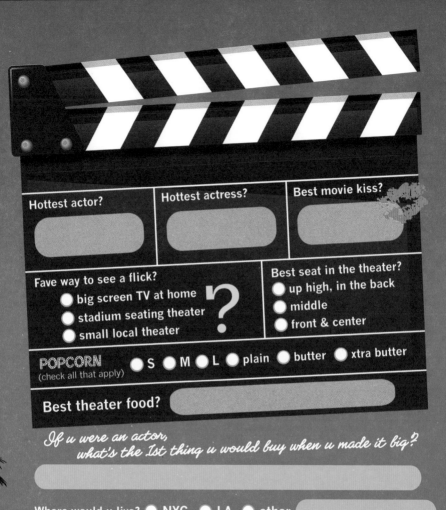

Hottest actor?

Hottest actress?

Best movie kiss?

Fave way to see a flick?
- ○ big screen TV at home
- ○ stadium seating theater
- ○ small local theater

?

Best seat in the theater?
- ○ up high, in the back
- ○ middle
- ○ front & center

POPCORN
(check all that apply)   ○ S ○ M ○ L ○ plain ○ butter ○ xtra butter

Best theater food?

If u were an actor,
what's the 1st thing u would buy when u made it big?

Where would u live? ○ **NYC** ○ **LA** ○ other

Like black & white movies?
○ yes ○ no

Ever watch a film w/ subtitles?
○ oui ○ no

Watch the Oscars?
○ yes ○ no

Best chick flick?
_____

If I had a band,

Name _____

1. **IF YOU HAD A BAND, WHAT WOULD U CALL IT?** _Girls Dck_

2. What's most fun to pop? ○ popcorn ● bubble wrap ○ balloons?

3. What's your screensaver? _____

4. Jeans with ○ flip-flops ○ flats ○ heels ● sneakers?

5. I *luv the sound* of _____.

6. Do straw slurping sounds bug u? ○ yes ● no

7. How 'bout nails on a chalkboard? ● yes ○ no

8. Hottest place u've ever been? _California_

9. **Coldest place u've ever been?** _Ohio_

10. Do u have ○ awful ○ OK ● great handwriting?

11. **ULTIMATE** romantic movie? _don't like them_

12. Who do you usually see movies with? _My Family_

13. ● Candlelight ○ Lamplight ○ Flashlight?

14. What do ur sunglasses look like? _____

15. ● **Country house** ○ Big city condo

16. Coolest person u know? _Jack_

17. Most stylish person u know? _Katie ava_

18. Funniest person u know? _Noha ?_

19. Most annoying? ○ bad breath ● smacking gum ○ talking with mouth full

20. *Something u say ur going 2 do but never do?* _____

DANCE HIP-HOP

I would name it after me.

Name _Redson_

1. SOMETHING U'D LUV TO WEAR BUT DON'T HAVE THE NERVE? _____

2. Scared 2 travel over tall bridges? ◯ oh yeah ◯ no way, it's safe

3. Ever had food poisoning? ◯ no ◯ yes. What did u eat? _____

4. Had an ant farm? ◯ yes ◯ no ◯ just the idea makes me sting!

5. Grown Sea-Monkeys®? ◯ oh yeah ◯ no ◯ what r those?

6. Who do u text the most? _____

7. Rescued a wild animal? ◯ no ◯ yes. What kind? _____

8. R u ticklish? ◯ YES! AHH! ◯ not really

9. ◯ From scratch ◯ from a box ◯ no mac & cheese?

10. I wish my family had a _____

11. Which is worst? ◯ Gnats ◯ Flies ◯ Mosquitoes?

12. Watch TV while u eat dinner? ◯ always ◯ sometimes ◯ never

13. *Magazine cover u would like to appear on?* _____

14. ◯ Fall asleep in ◯ Scared to death of the dentist's chair?

15. Take the road ◯ less travelled ◯ everyone else follows?

16. Any nervous habits? ◯ nope ◯ yes. What? _____

17. Can u do a backbend? ◯ yep ◯ no, ow!

18. ULTIMATE sundae ingredients? _____

19. *Can u tie a knot in a cherry stem with your tongue?* ◯ no ◯ yep ◯ huh?

20. What could u write a book about? _____

my tunes

Name _____

What r your top 3 fave bands?
1.
2.
3.

What r your top five fave songs?

_____
Title
_____ is perfect to dance to.

_____
Title
_____ is great to sing with.

_____
Title
_____ has the coolest lyrics.

_____
Title
_____ has awesome music.

_____
Title
_____ is the best overall song.

What's on ur playlist?
(check all that apply)
- rock
- pop
- alternative
- country
- dance
- rap/hip hop
- other _____

CONCERT IN A
⬤ BIG STADIUM ⬤ COOL DANCE CLUB ⬤ SMALL, INTIMATE CLUB?

SEEN ANYONE IN CONCERT? ⬤ NOPE ⬤ YEP. WHO?
_____

WHO R U DYING TO SEE IN CONCERT?
_____

my tunes

Coolest male singer?
_____

Hottest female singer?
_____

Best performer look?
- ◯ JEANS & A T-SHIRT
- ◯ SUPER GLAM
- ◯ ANYTHING + A COWBOY HAT

dance
- ◯ with friends
- ◯ alone in your house?
  (in front of a mirror?)
  - ◯ of course
  - ◯ no way!

Coolest lyrics from a song?

Lyrics
_____
_____
_____
_____

Song Title

OH

LAST ALBUM U BOUGHT?
_____
_____

◯ I don't buy ENTIRE Albums! I NEVER like ALL the songs.

the LINES?

Name Reagan

1. color in the lines? ○ no ● yes

2. How many pillows do you sleep with?

one

3. ● Team ○ Individual sports?

4. Can u read music? ○ yes ● no

5. What's worth waking up really early 4?

christmas morning

6. Believe in haunted houses? ○ yes, scary! ● no, it's all a hoax!

7. How about psychics? ○ yes ○ no, it's a scam

8. Swim in ● a pool (boring?) ○ a lake (alligators?) ○ the ocean (sharks?)

9. If u could only have 1 hobby, what would it be? art

10. Libraries r ● so cool ○ too quiet ○ OK, I guess

11. IF WE HAD 2 B NAMED AFTER PLANETS, WHICH WOULD U CHOOSE? Mars

12. How about a city? newyork

13. WHAT ABOUT A COLOR? violite

14. Chew on ice? ○ no way, that's bad 4 u ● oh yeah

15. Bird ever drop something (u know!) on u? ○ yes, gross! ● nope

16. Eakspa igpa atinla? ● WHAT?! ○ esya, Ia oda

17. ULTIMATE fried food? yes

18. Fave color to write with? ○ black ● blue ○ other

19. Send ○ really wordy ● super short text messages?

20. Ever drunk wheat grass? ● no ○ yes

How was it? I don't know

HOW BORING!

Name Reagan

nice

1. Color things the correct colors (GREEN GRASS, BLUE SKY)? ● yes ○ no, how boring!

2. ○ Cityscape ● Ocean sunset ○ Mountain view?

3. Won an award? ○ nah ● yes. What 4? Soccer

4. ○ Sweet ● Sour ○ Sweet & Sour?

5. ○ Store-bought ● Homemade Valentine?

6. Best food when it's cold outside? Hot dog

7. How about when it's hot? ice cream

8. ○ Big ● Medium ○ Little dogs?

9. ○ BLUSH ○ BUBBLEGUM ○ HOT ● NO PINK?

10. Meanest thing a sibling's done 2 u? Opend her presenten

11. Nicest thing a sibling's done 4 u? bot me a present

12. Sit ● up front ○ in the middle ○ in the back of class?

13. I could beat everyone in an arm wrestling match.

14. Ridden on a horse? ● yes ○ no

15. ULTIMATE TV network? ABC

16. Keep a diary? ● no ○ yes

17. Read someone else's diary? ● no, that's private! ○ yeah, I feel bad.

18. New Year's resolutions? ● no ○ yes. This year's? _____

19. MET A CELEBRITY? ● no ○ yes, Who? _____

20. How's your singing? ○ Awful! ● OK ○ Better than average ○ Awesome!

DESERT ISLAND

YOU ARE stranded on a remote island for 1 year....
make wise choices OR if u really want to laugh,
write down the 1st thing that comes to ur mind.

U can have one food item (besides ALL the fish you can catch!)
What would u choose?

Hotdog

1 BEVERAGE? (Besides fresh H20)

rootbear

What ONE outfit would U
bring to wear?

Top tanktop

Bottom Shorts

Shoes sneakers

1 AUTHOR
You get all the books they've ever written.

Dr. Suess

1 MAGAZINE
Don't worry, you'll get one a month!

1 FREEBIE ITEM — IT CAN BE ANYTHING . . .

but ur cell phone, most likely won't have good reception . . .
so think of something else.

I pod

While struggling to survive, what cool thing could u do for 1 whole year?

Swing on a vine

BEST THING ABOUT SOLO ISLAND LIVING?

- the beach
- ● do WHATEVER I want
- great tan
- lots of "alone" time

ICKIEST THING ABOUT
UR SO-CALLED PARADISE?

- too much alone time
- awful sunburn
- learning to fish
- ● SAND!! in everything!

U R FINALLY RESCUED!
YAY!

1st person u'd want to see?

Eve

1st thing u'd want to do? ➡ Play

1st thing u'd want to eat? ➡ cheeseburger

HELP!

Do U stare @ people?

Name _Rough_

1. Do U stare @ people? ○ No, how rude! ● Depends ○ Of course, I can't help it
2. Something u like. (1ST THING THAT COMES TO MIND): _Ace cream_
3. Something u dislike. (1ST THING THAT COMES TO MIND): _____
4. **Strawberry** ○ **shortcake** ● **milkshake** ○ **jam?**
5. IF U WERE FAMOUS, WHAT WOULD BE UR STAGE NAME? _____
6. Do u like hugging? ○ yes ○ not really, it invades my personal space
7. WHAT SPORT DO U REALLY STINK @? _____
8. Ever take ballet? ● **yes** ○ **no**
9. Watch sports on TV ? ○ **no way** ● **yes.** What? _Football_
10. Make any cool sound effects? ○ **nah** ● **yes.** What? _____
11. R u good at imitating people? ○ **no** ○ **sort of** ○ **yes**
12. Name of fave stuffed animal when u were a kid? _____
13. FUNNIEST aCTOR? _____._____
14. Stuck a piece of chewed gum somewhere? ○ **no, yuck!** ○ **yes.** _____
    ↖ where?
15. **ULTIMATE** CURE 4 hiccups? _____
16. **What's most important to u?** ○ looks ○ smarts ○ popularity ○ other_____
17. Ugliest shoes u've owned? _____
18. Spilled something on urself in public? ○ **no** ○ **yes.** What? _____
19. Spilled something on someone else? ○ **no** ○ **yes.** What? _____
20. Have a crush on someone? ○ **not right now** ● **yeah**

What do U think?

Name _Reagan Miele_

1. **PERFORMED IN FRONT OF AN AUDIENCE?** ◯ NO ☑ YES. WHAT 4? _Saturday_

2. **ULTIMATE** condiment? ◯ Mayo ☑ Mustard ◯ Ketchup ◯ All, mixed together

3. What mall store defines your personality? _Olympia_

4. 1 thing u argue about w/ parents? _____

5. Fold your underwear? ◯ yes ☑ **r u joking?**

6. ◯ It's hard ◯ I don't like ☑ I LUV to make new friends?

7. Something ur family does together that u LUV? _Floridia_

8. Something ur family does together that u can't stand? _Musems_

9. **HELD A BABY CHICK?** ◯ yep ☑ **nope**

10. Been in a parade? ◯ **no** ☑ yes. What didja do? _Walk_

11. Good @ solving mysteries in movies? ◯ **no** ☑ **yes**, I should be a detective!

12. **R U A FREAKY CHANNEL SURFER?** ◯ oh yeah ◯ **no, that's SO ANNOYING!**

13. Most creative thing u've done? _____

14. **WOULD U GIVE SOMEONE A PEDICURE?** ◯ **no, FEET R GROSS!** ◯ **sure.**

15. Jealous of a brother/sister? ◯ **no** ◯ **yes.** Y? _____

16. Do u brag? ◯ **no** ◯ **sure** ◯ **ugh, I think so**

17. Speak another language? ◯ **nope** ◯ yes. What? _____

18. **WOULD U RATHER** ◯ **GLOW IN THE DARK** ◯ **SHIMMER IN THE DAYLIGHT?**

19. Left an awful movie? ◯ **nah** ◯ **yes.** Name? _____

20. My 1st crush was _____ when I was _____ yrs. old.

1. SKELETONS ○ GIVE ME THE CREEPS! EW! ○ R SO COOL!

2. Fave game show? _____

3. Game show u think u MIGHT do well on? _____

4. ○ Strawberries ○ Bananas ○ Oranges ○ Apples
   ○ Pears ○ Other _____ ?

Name _____

5. Ever picked your own fruit/veggies from a farm?
   ○ NO ○ YES. What? _____

6. ○ Piano ○ Acoustic guitar ○ Electric guitar
   ○ Saxophone ○ Other _____?

7. I ○ can't stand being too busy
   ○ LUV having too much going on.

8. Embarrassing celebrity crush u had when you
   were younger? _____

9. Ever gone to camp? ○ NO ○ YES
   Name of it? _____

10. Want to be in politics?
   ○ Yeah, it would B really cool ○ R u kidding me?!

11. I stink at anything requiring ○ artistic ○ scientific skills.

12. ○ Klutzy ○ Perfectly coordinated?

13. ULTIMATE movie soundtrack? _____

14. Something u bought that u regret? _____

15. Grossest thing boys do? _____

16. I escape by ○ listening to music ○ watching TV
   ○ getting lost in a book ○ taking a nap.

17. SCARED 2 STAY ALONE IN UR HOUSE @ NIGHT? ○ ALWAYS ○ SOMETIMES ○ NOPE

18. Celebrity U would love 2 interview? _____

19. Nickname? ○ NO ○ YES. How'd u get it?
   _____

20. R U named after anyone? ○ NO ○ YES. Who? _____

1. Which is scariest? ○ **VAMPIRE** ○ **ZOMBIE** ○ WITCH ○ None, they're not real!

2. Last thing u watched on YouTube? _____

3. Ever been on YouTube? ○ **NO** ○ **YES**

4. Wish u had a twin? ○ no way! ○ yeah, that would b cool.

5. If ur BFF were a food, what would she/he be?

_____

6. Cops ○ make me feel safe ○ kinda scare me.

7. Seen a waterfall? ○ **NO** ○ **YES.** Which one(s)?

_____

8. ○ **MySpace** ○ **Facebook** ○ **other** _____ ?

9. I would LUV to be famous 4 _____

_____ .

10. If u had wings, where would u fly 2?

_____ Y? _____

11. If ur personality were a car, what would it be?

_____

12. READ UR HOROSCOPE? ○ YES, FOR FUN ○ NO, IT'S ALL MADE UP

13. ULTIMATE adventure w/ a friend? _____

_____

14. I mostly like to be around
○ funny ○ smart ○ warm-hearted people.

15. Make wishes & throw coins into fountains? ○ **YES** ○ **NAH**

16. I ○ like to please people ○ don't care what others think.

17. Eat sushi? ○ **NO, GROSS!** ○ **YES.** Fave kind? _____

_____

18. It's cooler to hang out with ○ girls ○ guys.

19. Something u believed as a little kid? _____

20. I think most people think I'm ○ funny ○ snobby ○ friendly ○ weird.

Name _____

style
conscious

I luv to shop for my clothes @
1. _____
2. _____
3. _____

Store u like 2 visit but usually don't buy from?

_____

Last accessory u bought?

_____

Do u own something
you've never worn?
⬭ No ⬭ Yes
What? _____

I

⬭ put a lot of thought
into what I wear.

⬭ throw my clothes on
quickly.

⬭ just like to be
comfortable.

If I could, I would wear _____ every day.

my closet is mostly full of
⬭ jeans ⬭ skirts ⬭ tops ⬭ other _____.

Most comfortable article of clothing I own is my
_____.

What hat would u never, ever wear?
- baseball cap
- cowboy hat
- beret
- other _____
- I would try any of them. I LUV hats!

What's ur style?

- preppy – smart, not opposed to plaid
- boho – romantic, billowy, artsy
- punk – edgy, crazy, rock 'n' roll
- diva – all glam, glitzy, probably like pink
- I don't fit into these molds! Then describe your style.

_____
_____
_____
_____
_____
_____
_____

my faves

T-shirt

Dress

Sweater

Shoes

Bag

Earrings

pick me

pick me

pick me

If you were a dog, what kind would u be?

NAME Reagan

1. If u were a dog, what kind would u be? Collie

2. Choose a secret agent name 4 yourself – black Widow

3. Which is worth it? ● mouth on FIRE from hot sauce ○ ice cream brain freeze ○ neither!

4. EAT M&M'S ® ○ 1 @ A TIME ○ BY THE HANDFUL?

5. Ever made a snow angel? ● YEP ○ NOPE ○ WHAT IS THAT?!

6. ULTIMATE part of a cake? ● cake ○ frosting ○ filling

7. ● Dancing ● Listening to music?

8. Ever complete a puzzle? ● YES ○ NO, HOW BORING!

9. What sweet food could u never, ever give up? Sour Patch Kids

10. I wish I could be paid to eat hot dogs .

11. HOW MANY TEETH dO U HAVE? _____

12. How many fillings do u have? Zero

13. Do toothpaste WORMS in the sink bug u? ○ YES! ● NO ○ WHAT?!

14. Ever been sent to the principal's office? ● NO ○ YES, what 4? _____

15. Is it worth being sick to miss school? ○ YEP ○ NOPE ● SOMETIMES

16. When do u make your bed? ○ a.m. ● when I'm told 2 ○ uh, never?

17. ○ Untie ● Kick off sneakers?

18. Ever take the blame 4 something someone else did? ○ YES ● NO

19. Ever blamed someone else 4 something u did? ● YES :(○ NO

20. Magical power u wish u had? Judy

don't even think about it

NAME _____

1. Would u rather be a ◯ cat & wash yourself ◯ dog & get a bath?

2. Something guys **LUV** that u just don't get? _____

3. ULTIMATE **WINTER** Olympic sport? _____

4. ULTIMATE *summer* Olympic sport? _____

5. Ever wear socks with holes in them? ◯ Sure, if they don't show ◯ NO!

6. I would **LUV** to take care of a ◯ baby ◯ puppy ◯ kitten.

7. Star ◯ gazing (as in the sky) ◯ watching (as in Hollywood)?

8. Open your mouth to put on mascara? ◯ YEAH, WEIRD ◯ NO ◯ DON'T WEAR IT

9. What's ur earliest memory? _____

10. Ever fed a goat? ◯ of course ◯ nah ◯ ew, no, don't they eat your clothes?

11. COOlest thing you've ever made by hand? _____

12. Singer whose songs u own the most of? _____

13. Spit out yucky food & ◯ hide in napkin ◯ put back on plate?

14. Afraid of public speaking? ◯ absolutely ◯ kind of ◯ nope

15. ◯ Grapes ◯ Raisins ◯ Neither?

16. What's under your bed? _____

17. EVER BEEN HYPNOTIZED? ◯ YES ◯ NO

18. Habit you'd want to break with hypnosis? _____

19. Concert you'd like a backstage pass 4? _____

20. **Celebrity crush u have?** _____

I wish mermaids were real

NAME _____

1. Something make-believe that u wish was real? _____

2. Something real that u wish was make-believe? _____

3. Last conversation I had was with _____ about _____.

4. Where do u do most of your heavy thinking? _____

5. Wash hair ◯ every day ◯ every other day ◯ twice a week?

6. ULTIMATE ROAD TRIP GAME? _____

7. ◯ Patient ◯ Impatient?

8. Something u own that would surprise friends? _____

9. ◯ Early ◯ On time ◯ Late person?

10. SOMETHING DUMB U DID AS A LITTLE KID? _____

11. Ever used a toothpick? ◯ yes, don't tell anyone ◯ No way

12. How do u wear your hair most of the time? _____

13. Ever gotten into poison ivy? ◯ yes! itchy! ◯ No

14. Ever dress up your pet? ◯ no pet :(◯ no! ◯ yes! With what? _____

15. **Talk during movies?** ◯ never ◯ sometimes a little ◯ always

16. Sing in the shower? ◯ No ◯ yes. How do u sound? _____

17. Scared of clowns? ◯ oh yeah ◯ nah

18. ◯ First ◯ Last to raise your hand in class?

19. ◯ Stick to plans ◯ Wing it?

20. R u a ◯ good ◯ great ◯ awful photographer?

Guitar Hero of course

NAMe _____

1. **ULTIMATE** video game? _____

2. Ever been seriously lost? ○ no ○ yes ↘
   What happened? _____

3. Friend ur similar 2? _____

4. Friend ur the exact opposite of? _____

5. How many pairs of jeans do u own? _____

6. Ever written a poem? ○ *No way* ○ *yes*

7. ○ Mexican ○ Chinese ○ Pizza?

8. Iron your clothes in the a.m.? ○ of course ○ r u kidding?

9. Know anyone u think can read ur mind? ○ *No* ○ *yes* ↘
   Who? _____

10. ○ **Chocolate mints** ○ **Mint gum** ○ **Hard mint candies?**

11. Your house is on fire!
    ↘ *What 1 item would u save?* _____

12. ○ Black
    ○ Refried beans?

13. ○ Cookies ○ Candy?

14. ○ Secret garden ○ Public park?

15. Own slippers? ○ *No* ○ *yes* ↘
    What do they look like? _____

16. R u most like ○ SpongeBob ○ Patrick ○ Squidward?

17. Most nutritious food u actually like to eat? _____

18. If u could only wear 1 outfit for 1 year
    ↘ *what would it be?* _____

19. Caught not paying attention in class? ○ no ○ of course!

20. Ever been grounded?
○ no ○ yes.
What 4? _____
_____

Star-Struck

Name _Reagan_

I would **LUV** to star opposite _Adam sandler_ actor _in a movie._

It would be so **Cool** to co-star with _ariana G_ actress _in a movie._

Fave movie character? _Roabuckt_

SCARIEST MOVIE MONSTER?

WORST MOVIE U'VE SEEN THIS YEAR?

the nutt Job

GRAND

BEST MOVIE U'VE SEEN THIS YEAR?

2 FAVE FLICK?

OK, # 3?

Y is it your Fave?

Hottest actor? Leonardo G.

Hottest actress? Ariana G.

Best movie kiss?

Fave way to see a flick?
- ● big screen TV at home
- ○ stadium seating theater
- ○ small local theater

Best seat in the theater?
- ○ up high, in the back
- ● middle
- ○ front & center

POPCORN (check all that apply)   ○ S   ● M   ○ L   ○ plain   ● butter   ○ xtra butter

Best theater food? Peanut E.M&'s

If u were an actor, what's the 1st thing u would buy when u made it big?
#1 Red Punchbuagie

Where would u live? ○ NYC   ○ LA   ● other   Florida

Like black & white movies?
○ yes ● no

Ever watch a film w/ subtitles?
○ oui ○ no

Watch the Oscars?
○ yes ● no

Best chick flick?
_____

If I had a band,

Name _____

1. **IF YOU HAD A BAND, WHAT WOULD U CALL IT?** _____

2. What's most fun to pop? ○ popcorn ● bubble wrap ○ balloons?

3. What's your screensaver? _____

4. Jeans with ○ flip-flops ○ flats ○ heels ○ sneakers?

5. I *luv the sound* of _____.

6. Do straw slurping sounds bug u? ○ yes ● no

7. How 'bout nails on a chalkboard? ● yes ○ no

8. Hottest place u've ever been? _____

9. Coldest place u've ever been? _____

10. Do u have ○ awful ○ OK ○ great handwriting?

11. **ULTIMATE** romantic movie? _____

12. Who do you usually see movies with? _____

13. ○ Candlelight ○ Lamplight ○ Flashlight?

14. What do ur sunglasses look like? _____

15. ○ **Country house** ○ Big city condo

16. Coolest person u know? _____

17. Most stylish person u know? _____

18. Funniest person u know? _____

19. Most annoying? ○ bad breath ○ smacking gum ○ talking with mouth full

20. Something u say ur going 2 do but never do? _____

DANCE HIP-HOP

I would name it after me.

Name _____

1. SOMETHING U'D LUV TO WEAR BUT DON'T HAVE THE NERVE? _____

2. Scared 2 travel over tall bridges? ○ oh yeah ● no way, it's safe

3. Ever had food poisoning? ○ no ● yes. What did u eat? big candy bar

4. Had an ant farm? ○ yes ● no ○ just the idea makes me sting!

5. Grown Sea-Monkeys®? ○ oh yeah ○ no ● what r those?

6. Who do u text the most? _____

7. Rescued a wild animal? ○ no ○ yes. What kind? _____

8. R u ticklish? ○ YES! AHH! ● not really

9. ○ From scratch ○ from a box ○ no mac & cheese?

10. I wish my family had a pool, justin bieber consert

11. Which is worst? ○ Gnats ○ Flies ○ Mosquitoes?

12. Watch TV while u eat dinner? ○ always ● sometimes ○ never

13. *Magazine cover u would like to appear on?* _____

14. ○ Fall asleep in ○ Scared to death of the dentist's chair?

15. Take the road ○ less travelled ○ everyone else follows?

16. Any nervous habits? ● nope ○ yes. What? _____

17. Can u do a backbend? ● yep ○ no, ow!

18. ULTIMATE sundae ingredients? _____

19. Can u tie a knot in a cherry stem with your tongue? ● no ○ yep ○ huh?

20. What could u write a book about? _____

my tunes

Name _____

What r your top 3 fave bands?
1. Justin bieber
2. 1D
3.

What r your top five fave songs?

GanGamstyle
Title _____ is perfect to dance to.

Come and get it
Title _____ is great to sing with.

I love it
Title _____ has the coolest lyrics.

Can't holdus
Title _____ has awesome music.

Beauty andabeat
Title _____ is the best overall song.

What's on ur playlist?
(check all that apply)
- ✓ rock
- ✓ pop
- ✓ alternative
- ✓ country
- ✓ dance
- ✓ rap/hip hop
- other _____

CONCERT IN A
◐ BIG STADIUM ○ COOL DANCE CLUB ○ SMALL, INTIMATE CLUB?

SEEN ANYONE IN CONCERT? ○ NOPE ✓ YEP. WHO?
_____

WHO R U DYING TO SEE IN CONCERT?
Justin bieber agin

my tunes

Coolest male singer?
Justin bieber

Hottest female singer?
_____

Best performer look?
- ☑ JEANS & A T-SHIRT
- ◯ SUPER GLAM
- ◯ ANYTHING + A COWBOY HAT

dance

- ☑ with friends
- ◯ alone in your house?
  (in front of a mirror?)
  - ◯ of course
  - ◯ no way!

Coolest lyrics
   from a song?

Lyrics _____

_____

_____

_____

Song Title

OH

LAST
ALBUM U
BOUGHT?

_____

_____

◯ I don't buy ENTIRE Albums! I NEVER like ALL the songs.

COLOR IN THE LINES?

Name Λ í ʃ (in greek)

1. color in the lines? ○ no ✓ yes

2. How many pillows do you sleep with?

___one___

3. ✓ Team ○ Individual sports?

4. Can u read music? ✓ yes ○ no

5. What's worth waking up really early 4?

___last dohnut___

6. Believe in haunted houses? ○ yes, scary! ✓ no, it's all a hoax!

7. How about psychics? ○ yes ✓ no, it's a scam

8. Swim in ✓ a pool (boring?) ○ a lake (alligators?) ○ the ocean (sharks?)

9. If u could only have 1 hobby, what would it be? ___sports___

10. Libraries r ○ so cool ○ too quiet ✓ OK, I guess

11. IF WE HAD 2 B NAMED AFTER PLANETS, WHICH WOULD U CHOOSE? ___Saturn___

12. How about a city? ___Hudson___

13. WHAt ABºUt A CºLºR? ___Violet___

14. Chew on ice? ○ no way, that's bad 4 u ✓ oh yeah

15. Bird ever drop something (u know!) on u? ○ yes, gross! ✓ nope

16. Eakspa igpa atinla? ✓ WHAT?! ○ esya, Ia oda

17. ULTIMATE fried food? ___funnel cake___

18. Fave color to write with? ○ black ○ blue ✓ other ___violet___

19. Send ✓ really wordy ○ super short text messages?

20. Ever drunk wheat grass? ✓ no ○ yes

How was it? _____

HOW BORING!

nice

Name RM 15

1. Color things the correct colors (GREEN GRASS, BLUE SKY)? ☑ **yes** ○ **no,** how boring!

2. ○ Cityscape ☑ Ocean sunset ○ Mountain view?

3. Won an award? ○ **nah** ☑ **yes.** What 4? won a mile

4. ○ Sweet ○ Sour ☑ Sweet & Sour?

5. ○ **Store-bought** ☑ **Homemade Valentine?**

6. Best food when it's cold outside? hamburger

7. How about when it's hot? ice cream

8. ☑ Big ○ Medium ○ Little dogs?

9. ○ **BLUSH** ○ **BUBBLEGUM** ☑ **HOT** ○ **NO PINK?**

10. *Meanest* thing a sibling's done 2 u? _____

11. *Nicest* thing a sibling's done 4 u? _____

12. Sit ☑ up front ○ in the middle ○ in the back of class?

13. **I could beat** Reese **in an arm wrestling match.**

14. Ridden on a horse? ☑ **yes** ○ **no**

15. **ULTIMATE TV network?** Naflix

16. Keep a diary? ○ **no** ☑ **yes**

17. Read someone else's diary? ○ **no,** that's private! ☑ **yeah,** I feel bad.

18. New Year's resolutions? ☑ **no** ○ **yes.** This year's? _____

19. **MET A CELEBRITY?** ○ **no** ☑ **yes,** Who? Megan Klinigberg's dad

20. How's your singing? ○ Awful! ☑ OK ○ Better than average ○ Awesome!

DESERT ISLAND

YOU ARE stranded on a remote island for 1 year . . .
make wise choices OR if u really want to laugh,
write down the 1st thing that comes to ur mind.

U can have one food item (besides ALL the fish you can catch!)
What would u choose?

> steak

1 BEVERAGE? (Besides fresh H2O)

> lemonade

What ONE outfit would U
bring to wear?

Top _swim shirt-_
I ♡ Beach
Bottom _jean_
capries
Shoes _sneakers_

1 AUTHOR
You get all the books they've ever written.

> J. K. Rowling

1 MAGAZINE
Don't worry, you'll get one a month!

> ?

1 FREEBIE ITEM — IT CAN BE ANYTHING . . .

but ur cell phone, most likely won't have good reception . . . so think of something else.

> beach towel

While struggling to survive, what cool thing could u do for 1 whole year?

> climb trees

BEST THING ABOUT SOLO ISLAND LIVING?

- ⬤ the beach
- ☑ do WHATEVER I want
- ⬤ great tan
- ⬤ lots of "alone" time

ICKIEST THING ABOUT UR SO-CALLED PARADISE?

- ☑ too much alone time
- ⬤ awful sunburn
- ⬤ learning to fish
- ⬤ SAND!! in everything!

U R FINALLY RESCUED! YAY!

1st person u'd want to see?

> Mom + dad

1st thing u'd want to do? ➡ sleep in bed

HELP!

1st thing u'd want to eat? ➡ salad

Do U stare @ people?

1. **Do U stare @ people?** ○ No, how rude! ○ Depends ○ Of course, I can't help it

2. Something u like. (1ST THING THAT COMES TO MIND): _____

3. Something u dislike. (1ST THING THAT COMES TO MIND): _____

4. **Strawberry** ○ **shortcake** ○ **milkshake** ○ **jam?**

5. IF U WERE FAMOUS, WHAT WOULD BE UR STAGE NAME? _____

6. Do u like hugging? ○ yes ○ not really, it invades my personal space

7. WHAT SPORT DO U REALLY STINK @?_____

8. Ever take ballet? ○ **yes** ○ **no**

9. Watch sports on TV ? ○ **no way** ○ **yes.** What? _____

10. Make any cool sound effects? ○ **nah** ○ **yes.** What? _____

11. R u good at imitating people? ○ **no** ○ **sort of** ○ **yes**

12. Name of fave stuffed animal when u were a kid? _____

13. FUNNIEST ACTOR? _____

14. Stuck a piece of chewed gum somewhere? ○ **no, yuck!** ○ **yes.** _____
↖where?

15. **ULTIMATE** CURE 4 hiccups? _____

16. **What's most important to u?** ○ looks ○ smarts ○ popularity ○ other_____

17. **Ugliest shoes u've owned?** _____

18. Spilled something on urself in public? ○ **no** ○ **yes.** What? _____

19. Spilled something on someone else? ○ **no** ○ **yes.** What? _____

20. Have a crush on someone? ○ **not right now** ○ **yeah**

What do U think?

Name _____

1. PERFORMED IN FRONT OF AN AUDIENCE? ◯ NO ◯ YES. WHAT 4? _____

2. ULTIMATE condiment? ◯ Mayo ◯ Mustard ◯ Ketchup ◯ All, mixed together

3. What mall store defines your personality? _____

4. 1 thing u argue about w/ parents? _____

5. Fold your underwear? ◯ yes ◯ r u joking?

6. ◯ It's hard ◯ I don't like ◯ I LUV to make new friends?

7. Something ur family does together that u LUV? _____

8. Something ur family does together that u can't stand? _____

9. HELD A BABY CHICK? ◯ yep ◯ nope

10. Been in a parade? ◯ no ◯ yes. What didja do? _____

11. Good @ solving mysteries in movies? ◯ no ◯ yes, I should be a detective!

12. R U A FREAKY CHANNEL SURFER? ◯ oh yeah ◯ no, that's SO ANNOYING!

13. Most creative thing u've done? _____

14. WOULD U GIVE SOMEONE A PEDICURE? ◯ no, FEET R GROSS! ◯ sure.

15. Jealous of a brother/sister? ◯ no ◯ yes. Y? _____

16. Do u brag? ◯ no ◯ sure ◯ ugh, I think so

17. Speak another language? ◯ nope ◯ yes. What? _____

18. WOULD U RATHER ◯ GLOW IN THE DARK ◯ SHIMMER IN THE DAYLIGHT?

19. Left an awful movie? ◯ nah ◯ yes. Name? _____

20. My 1st crush was _____ when I was _____ yrs. old.

1. SKELETONS ⚪ GIVE ME THE CREEPS! EW! ⚪ R SO COOL!

2. Fave game show? _____

3. Game show u think u MIGHT do well on?_____

4. ⚪ Strawberries ⚪ Bananas ⚪ Oranges ⚪ Apples
   ⚪ Pears ⚪ Other _____ ?

NaMe _____

5. Ever picked your own fruit/veggies from a farm?
   ⚪ NO ⚪ YES. What? _____

6. ⚪ Piano ⚪ Acoustic guitar ⚪ Electric guitar
   ⚪ Saxophone ⚪ Other _____?

7. I ⚪ can't stand being too busy
   ⚪ LUV having too much going on.

8. Embarrassing celebrity crush u had when you
   were younger? _____

9. Ever gone to camp? ⚪ NO ⚪ YES
   Name of it? _____

10. Want to be in politics?
    ⚪ Yeah, it would B really cool ⚪ R u kidding me?!

11. I stink at anything requiring ⚪ artistic ⚪ scientific skills.

12. ⚪ Klutzy ⚪ Perfectly coordinated?

13. ULTIMATE movie soundtrack? _____

14. Something u bought that u regret? _____

15. Grossest thing boys do? _____

16. I escape by ⚪ listening to music ⚪ watching TV
    ⚪ getting lost in a book ⚪ taking a nap.

17. SCARED 2 STAY ALONE IN UR HOUSE @ NIGHT? ⚪ ALWAYS ⚪ SOMETIMES ⚪ NOPE

18. Celebrity U would love 2 interview? _____

19. Nickname? ⚪ NO ⚪ YES. How'd u get it?
    _____

20. R U named after anyone? ⚪ NO ⚪ YES. Who?_____

1. Which is scariest? ◯ **VAMPIRE** ◯ **ZOMBIE** ◯ WITCH ◯ None, they're not real!

2. Last thing u watched on YouTube? _____

3. Ever been on YouTube? ◯ **NO** ◯ **YES**

4. Wish u had a twin? ◯ no way! ◯ yeah, that would b cool.

5. If ur BFF were a food, what would she/he be?
_____

6. Cops ◯ make me feel safe ◯ kinda scare me.

7. Seen a waterfall? ◯ **NO** ◯ **YES.** Which one(s)?
_____

8. ◯ **MySpace** ◯ **Facebook** ◯ **other** _____?

9. I would LUV to be famous 4 _____
_____.

10. If u had wings, where would u fly 2?
_____ Y? _____

11. If ur personality were a car, what would it be?
_____

12. READ UR HOROSCOPE? ◯ YES, FOR FUN ◯ NO, IT'S ALL MADE UP

13. **ULTIMATE adventure w/ a friend?** _____
_____

14. I mostly like to be around
◯ funny ◯ smart ◯ warm-hearted people.

15. Make wishes & throw coins into fountains? ◯ **YES** ◯ **NAH**

16. I ◯ like to please people ◯ don't care what others think.

17. Eat sushi? ◯ **NO, GROSS!** ◯ **YES.** Fave kind? _____
_____

18. It's cooler to hang out with ◯ girls ◯ guys.

19. Something u believed as a little kid? _____

20. I think most people think I'm ◯ funny ◯ snobby ◯ friendly ◯ weird.

style
conscious

Name _REM_

I luv to shop for my clothes @
1. _justice_
2. _target_
3. _old navy_

Store u like 2 visit but usually don't buy from?

Nicky Nicole

Last accessory u bought?

Purse

Do u own something
you've never worn?
⬤ No ⬤ Yes
What? _____

I

⬤ put a lot of thought
into what I wear.

⬤ throw my clothes on
quickly.

⬤ just like to be
comfortable.

If I could, I would wear _____ every day.

my closet is mostly full of
⬤ jeans ⬤ skirts ⬤ tops ⬤ other _____.

Most comfortable article of clothing I own is my

_____.

What hat would u never, ever wear?
- baseball cap
- cowboy hat
- beret
- other _____
- I would try any of them. I LUV hats!

What's ur style?

- preppy – smart, not opposed to plaid
- boho – romantic, billowy, artsy
- punk – edgy, crazy, rock 'n' roll
- diva – all glam, glitzy, probably like pink
- I don't fit into these molds! Then describe your style.

  _____
  _____
  _____
  _____
  _____
  _____
  _____

my faves

T-shirt

Dress

Sweater

Shoes

Bag

Earrings

pick me

pick me

pick me

If you were a dog, what kind would u be?

NAME Reagan

1. If u were a dog, what kind would u be? grey hound

2. Choose a secret agent name 4 yourself – pig sout 94

3. Which is worth it? ○ mouth on FIRE from hot sauce ● ice cream brain freeze ○ neither!

4. **eAt M&M'S** ® ○ 1 @ A time ○ BY the HANDFUL?

5. Ever made a snow angel? ● YEP ○ NOPE ○ WHAT IS THAT?!

6. ULTIMATE part of a cake? ● cake ○ frosting ○ filling

7. ● Dancing ○ Listening to music?

8. Ever complete a puzzle? ● YES ○ NO, HOW BORING!

9. What sweet food could u never, ever give up? ice cream

10. I wish I could be paid to write neat cursive .

11. HOW MANY TEETH do U HAVe? dont count

12. How many fillings do u have? no fillinings

13. Do toothpaste W°RMS in the sink bug u? ● YES! ○ NO ○ WHAT?!

14. **Ever been sent to the principal's office?** ● NO ○ YES, what 4? _____

15. Is it worth being sick to miss school? ○ YEP ○ NOPE ● SOMETIMES

16. When do u make your bed? ○ a.m. ● when I'm told 2 ○ uh, never?

17. ○ Untie ● Kick off sneakers?

18. Ever take the blame 4 something someone else did? ○ YES ● NO

19. Ever blamed someone else 4 something u did? ● YES :(○ NO

20. **Magical power u wish u had?** to fly

don't even think about it

NAME Reagan

1. Would u rather be a ○ cat & wash yourself ☑ dog & get a bath?

2. Something guys **LUV** that u just don't get? _Eating things of ground_

3. ULTIMATE **WINTER** Olympic sport? _skiing_

4. ULTIMATE ʃummer Olympic sport? _Soccer_

5. Ever wear socks with holes in them? ☑ Sure, if they don't show ○ NO!

6. I would **LUV** to take care of a ○ baby ○ puppy ☑ kitten.

7. Star ○ gazing (as in the sky) ☑ watching (as in Hollywood)?

8. Open your mouth to put on mascara? ○ YEAH, WEIRD ○ NO ☑ DON'T WEAR IT

9. What's ur earliest memory? _don't know_

10. Ever fed a goat? ☑ of course ○ nah ○ ew, no, don't they eat your clothes?

11. COOlest thing you've ever made by hand? _clay toy_

12. Singer whose songs u own the most of? _Katy perry_

13. Spit out yucky food & ☑ hide in napkin ○ put back on plate?

14. Afraid of public speaking? ○ absolutely ☑ kind of ○ nope

15. ☑ Grapes ○ Raisins ○ Neither?

16. What's under your bed? _junk_

17. EVER BEEN HYPNOTIZED? ○ YES ☑ NO

18. Habit you'd want to break with hypnosis? _chewing on hair_

19. Concert you'd like a backstage pass 4? _Katy perry_

20. **Celebrity crush u have?** _no one_

I wish mermaids were real

NAME _____

1. Something make-believe that u wish was real? _____

2. Something real that u wish was make-believe? _____

3. Last conversation I had was with _____ about _____.

4. Where do u do most of your heavy thinking? _____

5. Wash hair ◯ every day ◯ every other day ◯ twice a week?

6. **ULTIMATE ROAD TRIP GAME?** _____

7. ◯ Patient ◯ Impatient?

8. Something u own that would surprise friends? _____

9. ◯ Early ◯ On time ◯ Late person?

10. SOMETHING DUMB U DID AS A LITTLE KID? _____

11. Ever used a toothpick? ◯ yes, don't tell anyone ◯ no way

12. How do u wear your hair most of the time? _____

13. Ever gotten into poison ivy? ◯ yes! itchy! ◯ no

14. Ever dress up your pet? ◯ no pet :(◯ no! ◯ yes! With what? _____

15. **Talk during movies?** ◯ never ◯ sometimes a little ◯ always

16. Sing in the shower? ◯ no ◯ yes. How do u sound? _____

17. Scared of clowns? ◯ oh yeah ◯ nah

18. ◯ First ◯ Last to raise your hand in class?

19. ◯ Stick to plans ◯ Wing it?

20. R u a ◯ good ◯ great ◯ awful photographer?

Guitar Hero® of course

NAme **RM**

1. **ULTIMATE** video game? **MC**

2. Ever been seriously lost? ○ no ○ yes
   What happeNed? **HULWIWG**

3. Friend ur similar 2? **K**

4. Friend ur the exact opposite of? **A&A ?**

5. How many pairs of jeans do u own? **?**

6. Ever written a poem? ○ **No way** ✓○ yes

7. ✓○ Mexican ○ Chinese ○ Pizza?

8. Iron your clothes in the a.m.? ○ of course ✓○ r u kidding?

9. Know anyone u think can read ur mind? ✓ **No** ○ yes
   Who? ✓

10. ○ Chocolate mints ✓○ Mint gum ○ Hard mint candies?

11. Your house is on fire!
    What 1 item would u save?

12. ○ Black
    ○ Refried beans?

13. ○ Cookies ✓○ Candy?

14. ○ Secret garden ✓○ Public park?

15. Own slippers? ○ **No** ✓○ yes
    What do they look like? ✓ **Boots**

16. R u most like ○ SpongeBob ✓○ Patrick ○ Squidward?

17. Most nutritious food u actually like to eat? **OF**

18. If u could only wear 1 outfit for 1 year
    what would it be? **JRS&SN**

19. Caught not paying attention in class? ○ no ✓○ of course!

20. Ever been grounded?
○ no ○ yes.
What 4? _____

Star-Struck

Name Reagan

I would **LUV** to star opposite Adam sandler (actor) in a movie.

It would be so **Cool** to co-star with Ariana grande (actress) in a movie.

Fave movie character?

SCARIEST MOVIE MONSTER?

WORST MOVIE U'VE SEEN THIS YEAR?

BEST MOVIE U'VE SEEN THIS YEAR?

 # 2 FAVE FLICK?

OK, # 3?

GRAND

Y is it your Fave?

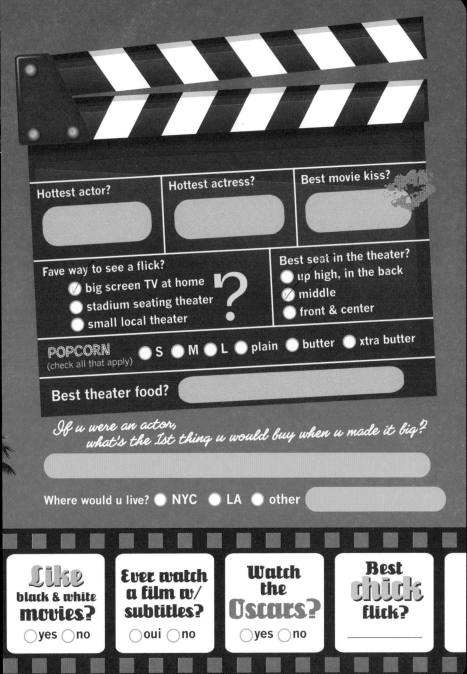

Hottest actor?

Hottest actress?

Best movie kiss?

Fave way to see a flick?
- ✓ big screen TV at home
- ○ stadium seating theater
- ○ small local theater

Best seat in the theater?
- ○ up high, in the back
- ✓ middle
- ○ front & center

POPCORN
(check all that apply)
○ S ○ M ○ L ○ plain ● butter ○ xtra butter

Best theater food?

If u were an actor, what's the 1st thing u would buy when u made it big?

Where would u live? ● NYC ● LA ● other

Like black & white movies?
○ yes ○ no

Ever watch a film w/ subtitles?
○ oui ○ no

Watch the Oscars?
○ yes ○ no

Best chick flick?
_____

ROCK POP

If I had a band,

Name _____

1. IF YOU HAD A BAND, WHAT WOULD U CALL IT? _____

2. What's most fun to pop? ○ popcorn ○ bubble wrap ○ balloons?

3. What's your screensaver? _____

4. Jeans with ○ flip-flops ○ flats ○ heels ○ sneakers?

5. *I luv the sound of* _____.

6. Do straw slurping sounds bug u? ○ yes ○ no

7. How 'bout nails on a chalkboard? ○ yes ○ no

8. Hottest place u've ever been? _____

9. Coldest place u've ever been? _____

10. Do u have ○ awful ○ OK ○ great handwriting?

11. ULTIMATE romantic movie? _____

12. Who do you usually see movies with? _____

13. ○ Candlelight ○ Lamplight ○ Flashlight?

14. What do ur sunglasses look like? _____

15. ○ **Country house** ○ Big city condo

16. Coolest person u know? _____

17. Most stylish person u know? _____

18. Funniest person u know? _____

19. Most annoying? ○ bad breath ○ smacking gum ○ talking with mouth full

20. *Something u say ur going 2 do but never do?* _____

I would name it after me.

Name _____

1. SOMETHING U'D LUV TO WEAR BUT DON'T HAVE THE NERVE? _____

2. Scared 2 travel over tall bridges? ○ oh yeah ○ no way, it's safe

3. Ever had food poisoning? ○ no ○ yes. What did u eat? _____

4. Had an ant farm? ○ yes ○ no ○ just the idea makes me sting!

5. Grown Sea-Monkeys®? ○ oh yeah ○ no ○ what r those?

6. Who do u text the most? _____

7. Rescued a wild animal? ○ no ○ yes. What kind? _____

8. R u ticklish? ○ YES! AHH! ○ not really

9. ○ From scratch ○ from a box ○ no mac & cheese?

10. I wish my family had a _____

11. Which is worst? ○ Gnats ○ Flies ○ Mosquitoes?

12. Watch TV while u eat dinner? ○ always ○ sometimes ○ never

13. Magazine cover u would like to appear on? _____

14. ○ Fall asleep in ○ Scared to death of the dentist's chair?

15. Take the road ○ less travelled ○ everyone else follows?

16. Any nervous habits? ○ nope ○ yes. What? _____

17. Can u do a backbend? ○ yep ○ no, ow!

18. ULTIMATE sundae ingredients? _____

19. Can u tie a knot in a cherry stem with your tongue? ○ no ○ yep ○ huh?

20. What could u write a book about? _____

my tunes

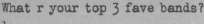

Name _____

What r your top 3 fave bands?
1.
2.
3.

What r your top five fave songs?

_____
Title
_____ is perfect to dance to.

_____
Title
_____ is great to sing with.

_____
Title
_____ has the coolest lyrics.

_____
Title
_____ has awesome music.

_____
Title
_____ is the best overall song.

What's on ur playlist?
(check all that apply)

- rock
- pop
- alternative
- country
- dance
- rap/hip hop
- other _____

CONCERT IN A
BIG STADIUM   COOL DANCE CLUB   SMALL, INTIMATE CLUB?

SEEN ANYONE IN CONCERT?   NOPE   YEP. WHO?
_____

WHO R U DYING TO SEE IN CONCERT?
_____

my Tunes

Coolest male singer?
_____

Hottest female singer?
_____

Best performer look?
◯ JEANS & A T-SHIRT
◯ SUPER GLAM
◯ ANYTHING + A COWBOY HAT

dance
◯ with friends
◯ alone in your house?
  (in front of a mirror?)
  ◯ of course
  ◯ no way!

Coolest lyrics from a song?

Lyrics _____

_____

_____

_____

_____

[Song Title]

OH

LAST
ALBUM U
BOUGHT?

_____

_____

◯ I don't buy ENTIRE Albums! I NEVER like ALL the songs.

COLOR IN THE LINES?

Name _Reagan_

1. color in the lines? ○ no ● yes

2. How many pillows do you sleep with?
one

3. ● Team ○ Individual sports?

4. Can u read music? ○ yes ● no

5. What's worth waking up really early 4?
soccer games

6. Believe in haunted houses? ○ yes, scary! ● no, it's all a hoax!

7. How about psychics? ○ yes ○ no, it's a scam

8. Swim in ● a pool (boring?) ○ a lake (alligators?) ○ the ocean (sharks?)

9. If u could only have 1 hobby, what would it be? _sports_

10. Libraries r ○ so cool ○ too quiet ● OK, I guess

11. IF WE HAD 2 B NAMED AFTER PLANETS, WHICH WOULD U CHOOSE? _Jupiter_

12. How about a city? _new york_

13. WHAt ABºUt A CºLºR? _violet_

14. Chew on ice? ○ no way, that's bad 4 u ● oh yeah

15. Bird ever drop something (u know!) on u? ○ yes, gross! ● nope

16. Eakspa igpa atinla? ● WHAT?! ○ esya, Ia oda

17. ULTIMATE fried food? _French fries_

18. Fave color to write with? ○ black ● blue ○ other _____

19. Send ○ really wordy ● super short text messages?

20. Ever drunk wheat grass? ● no ○ yes
How was it? _____

HOW BORING!

Name _Reagan_

nice

1. Color things the correct colors (GREEN GRASS, BLUE SKY)? ● yes ○ no, how boring!

2. ○ Cityscape ● Ocean sunset ○ Mountain view?

3. Won an award? ○ nah ● yes. What 4? _Macaroni Mile_

4. ○ Sweet ● Sour ○ Sweet & Sour?

5. ○ Store-bought ● Homemade Valentine?

6. Best food when it's cold outside? _chicken noodle soup_

7. How about when it's hot? _Ice cream_

8. ● Big ○ Medium ○ Little dogs?

9. ○ BLUSH ○ BUBBLEGUM ● HOT ○ NO PINK?

10. Meanest thing a sibling's done 2 u? _I dont Know_

11. Nicest thing a sibling's done 4 u? _I don't Know_

12. Sit ● up front ○ in the middle ○ in the back of class?

13. I could beat _all boys in class_ in an arm wrestling match.

14. Ridden on a horse? ● yes ○ no

15. ULTIMATE TV network? _Thundermans_

16. Keep a diary? ● no ○ yes

17. Read someone else's diary? ○ no, that's private! ● yeah, I feel bad.

18. New Year's resolutions? ● no ○ yes. This year's? _____

19. MET A CELEBRITY? ○ no ● yes, Who? _ME_

20. How's your singing? ○ Awful! ● OK ○ Better than average ○ Awesome!

DESERT ISLAND

YOU ARE stranded on a remote island for 1 year...
make wise choices OR if u really want to laugh,
write down the 1st thing that comes to ur mind.

U can have one food item (besides ALL the fish you can catch!)
What would u choose?

Salad with ranch dresing

1 BEVERAGE? (Besides fresh H20)

Gatorade

What ONE outfit would U
bring to wear?

Top _Tank top_
Hot Pink
Bottom _Jean_
shorts
Shoes _tenis shoes_

1 AUTHOR
You get all the books they've ever written.

JK Rowling

1 MAGAZINE
Don't worry, you'll get one a month!

 I dont know

1 FREEBIE ITEM — IT CAN BE ANYTHING . . .

but ur cell phone, most likely won't have good reception . . .
so think of something else.

Cooler

While struggling to survive, what cool thing could u do for 1 whole year?

go to the beach

BEST THING ABOUT SOLO ISLAND LIVING?

- the beach
- ● do WHATEVER I want
- great tan
- lots of "alone" time

ICKIEST THING ABOUT
UR SO-CALLED PARADISE?

- ● too much alone time
- awful sunburn
- learning to fish
- SAND!! in everything!

U R FINALLY RESCUED!
YAY!

1st person u'd want to see?

Ava

1st thing u'd want to do? → See my family

1st thing u'd want to eat? → Hot Dog

HELP!

Do U stare @ people?

Name _REM_

1. Do U stare @ people? ○ No, how rude! ⊘ Depends ○ Of course, I can't help it

2. Something u like. (1ST THING THAT COMES TO MIND): _jigs_

3. Something u dislike. (1ST THING THAT COMES TO MIND): _Sweet goatators_

4. **Strawberry** ○ **shortcake** ⊘ **milkshake** ○ **jam?**

5. IF U WERE FAMOUS, WHAT WOULD BE UR STAGE NAME? _Kit Kat_

6. Do u like hugging? ⊘ yes ○ not really, it invades my personal space

7. WHAT SPORT DO U REALLY STINK @? _gymnastics_

8. Ever take ballet? ⊘ **yes** ○ **no**

9. Watch sports on TV? ○ **no way** ⊘ **yes.** What? _football - b b_

10. Make any cool sound effects? ⊘ **nah** ○ **yes.** What? _____

11. R u good at imitating people? ○ **no** ○ **sort of** ○ **yes**

12. Name of fave stuffed animal when u were a kid? _bunny_

13. FUNNIEST ACTOR? _adam sandler_

14. Stuck a piece of chewed gum somewhere? ○ **no, yuck!** ○ **yes.** _____
↖where?

15. **ULTIMATE** CURE 4 hiccups? _____

16. **What's most important to u?** ○ **looks** ○ **smarts** ○ **popularity** ○ **other**_____

17. **Ugliest shoes u've owned?** _____

18. Spilled something on urself in public? ○ **no** ○ **yes.** What? _____

19. Spilled something on someone else? ○ **no** ○ **yes.** What? _____

20. Have a crush on someone? ○ **not right now** ○ **yeah**

What do U think?

Name _____

1. PERFORMED IN FRONT OF AN AUDIENCE? ○ NO ○ YES. WHAT 4? _____

2. ULTIMATE condiment? ○ Mayo ○ Mustard ○ Ketchup ○ All, mixed together

3. What mall store defines your personality? _____

4. 1 thing u argue about w/ parents? _____

5. Fold your underwear? ○ yes ○ r u joking?

6. ○ It's hard ○ I don't like ○ I LUV to make new friends?

7. Something ur family does together that u LUV? _____

8. Something ur family does together that u can't stand? _____

9. HELD A BABY CHICK? ○ yep ○ nope

10. Been in a parade? ○ no ○ yes. What didja do? _____

11. Good @ solving mysteries in movies? ○ no ○ yes, I should be a detective!

12. R U A FREAKY CHANNEL SURFER? ○ oh yeah ○ no, that's SO ANNOYING!

13. Most creative thing u've done? _____

14. WOULD U GIVE SOMEONE A PEDICURE? ○ no, FEET R GROSS! ○ sure.

15. Jealous of a brother/sister? ○ no ○ yes. Y? _____

16. Do u brag? ○ no ○ sure ○ ugh, I think so

17. Speak another language? ○ nope ○ yes. What? _____

18. WOULD U RATHER ○ GLOW IN THE DARK ○ SHIMMER IN THE DAYLIGHT?

19. Left an awful movie? ○ nah ○ yes. Name? _____

20. My 1st crush was _____ when I was _____ yrs. old.

1. SKELETONS ○ GIVE ME THE CREEPS! EW! ● R SO COOL!

2. Fave game show? win loose or draw

3. Game show u think u MIGHT do well on? win loose

4. ○ Strawberries ○ Bananas ○ Oranges ● Apples
   ○ Pears ○ Other _____ ?

   NAME _____

5. Ever picked your own fruit/veggies from a farm?
   ○ NO ● YES. What? apple

6. ○ Piano ○ Acoustic guitar ● Electric guitar
   ○ Saxophone ○ Other _____?

7. I ● can't stand being too busy
   ○ LUV having too much going on.

8. Embarrassing celebrity crush u had when you
   were younger? JB

9. Ever gone to camp? ○ NO ● YES
   Name of it? Mary Manor

10. Want to be in politics?
    ○ Yeah, it would B really cool ○ R u kidding me?!

11. I stink at anything requiring ● artistic ○ scientific skills.

12. ● Klutzy ○ Perfectly coordinated?

13. ULTIMATE movie soundtrack? _____

14. Something u bought that u regret? _____

15. Grossest thing boys do? Fart

16. I escape by ○ listening to music ● watching TV
    ○ getting lost in a book ○ taking a nap.

17. SCARED 2 STAY ALONE IN UR HOUSE @ NIGHT? ○ ALWAYS ● SOMETIMES ○ NOPE

18. Celebrity U would love 2 interview? Adam Sandler

19. Nickname? ● NO ○ YES. How'd u get it?

    _____

20. R U named after anyone? ○ NO ● YES. Who? Ronald Reagan

1. Which is scariest? ○ *VAMPIRE* ● **ZOMBIE** ○ WITCH ○ None, they're not real!

2. Last thing u watched on YouTube? _____

3. Ever been on YouTube? ○ **NO** ● **YES**

4. Wish u had a twin? ○ no way! ● yeah, that would b cool.

5. If ur BFF were a food, what would she/he be?
chiken leg

6. Cops ● make me feel safe ○ kinda scare me.

7. Seen a waterfall? ○ **NO** ● **YES.** Which one(s)?
_____

8. ○ **MySpace** ○ **Facebook** ○ **other** _____?

9. I would LUV to be famous 4 _____
_____.

10. If u had wings, where would u fly 2?
_____ Y? _____

11. If ur personality were a car, what would it be?
_____

12. READ UR HOROSCOPE? ○ YES, FOR FUN ○ NO, IT'S ALL MADE UP

13. **ULTIMATE adventure w/ a friend?** _____
_____

14. I mostly like to be around
○ funny ○ smart ○ warm-hearted people.

15. Make wishes & throw coins into fountains? ○ **YES** ○ **NAH**

16. I ○ like to please people ○ don't care what others think.

17. Eat sushi? ○ **NO, GROSS!** ○ **YES.** Fave kind? _____
_____

18. It's cooler to hang out with ○ girls ○ guys.

19. Something u believed as a little kid? _____

20. I think most people think I'm ○ funny ○ snobby ○ friendly ○ weird.

style
conscious

Name _____

I luv to shop for my clothes @
1. _____
2. _____
3. _____

Store u like 2 visit but usually don't buy from?

_____

Last accessory u bought?

_____

Do u own something
you've never worn?
⬤ No ⬤ Yes
What? _____

I

⬤ put a lot of thought
into what I wear.

⬤ throw my clothes on
quickly.

⬤ just like to be
comfortable.

If I could, I would wear _____ every day.

my closet is mostly full of
⬤ jeans ⬤ skirts ⬤ tops ⬤ other _____.

Most comfortable article of clothing I own is my
_____.

What hat would u never, ever wear?
- baseball cap
- cowboy hat
- beret
- other _____
- I would try any of them. I LUV hats!

What's ur style?

- preppy – smart, not opposed to plaid
- boho – romantic, billowy, artsy
- punk – edgy, crazy, rock 'n' roll
- diva – all glam, glitzy, probably like pink
- I don't fit into these molds! Then describe your style. ↘

_____
_____
_____
_____
_____
_____
_____

my faves

T-shirt

Dress

Sweater

Shoes

Bag

Earrings

pick me

pick me

pick me

If you were a dog, what kind would u be?

NAME Reagan

1. If u were a dog, what kind would u be? Grey hound

2. Choose a secret agent name 4 yourself – black widow

3. Which is worth it? ◯ mouth on FIRE from hot sauce ✓ ice cream brain freeze ◯ neither!

4. EAT M&M'S ® ◯ 1 @ A time ✓ BY the HANDFUL?

5. Ever made a snow angel? ✓ YEP ◯ NOPE ◯ WHAT IS THAT?!

6. ULTIMATE part of a cake? ✓ cake ◯ frosting ◯ filling

7. ✓ Dancing ◯ Listening to music?

8. Ever complete a puzzle? ✓ YES ◯ NO, HOW BORING!

9. What sweet food could u never, ever give up? chocolate

10. I wish I could be paid to play soccer.

11. HOW MANY TEETH do U Have? I don't know?

12. How many fillings do u have? None

13. Do toothpaste WORMS in the sink bug u? ✓ YES! ◯ NO ◯ WHAT?!

14. Ever been sent to the principal's office? ✓ NO ◯ YES, what 4?

15. Is it worth being sick to miss school? ◯ YEP ◯ NOPE ✓ SOMETIMES

16. When do u make your bed? ◯ a.m. ✓ when I'm told 2 ◯ uh, never?

17. ◯ Untie ✓ Kick off sneakers?

18. Ever take the blame 4 something someone else did? ◯ YES ✓ NO

19. Ever blamed someone else 4 something u did? ✓ YES :(◯ NO

20. Magical power u wish u had? Invisability

don't even think about it

NAME Reagan

1. Would u rather be a ✓ cat & wash yourself ○ dog & get a bath?

2. Something guys **LUV** that u just don't get? say whatever don't care

3. **ULTIMATE WINTER Olympic sport?** skiing

4. **ULTIMATE summer Olympic sport?** track

5. Ever wear socks with holes in them? ○ Sure, if they don't show ✓ NO!

6. I would **LUV** to take care of a ○ baby ○ puppy ○ kitten.

7. Star ○ gazing (as in the sky) ✓ watching (as in Hollywood)?

8. Open your mouth to put on mascara? ○ YEAH, WEIRD ○ NO ✓ DON'T WEAR IT

9. What's ur earliest memory? middle of some book was a lake

10. Ever fed a goat? ○ of course ○ nah ○ ew, no, don't they eat your clothes?

11. **COOLEST** thing you've ever made by hand? Juck tap pig

12. Singer whose songs u own the most of? Justin Bieber

13. Spit out yucky food & ✓ hide in napkin ○ put back on plate?

14. Afraid of public speaking? ○ absolutely ✓ kind of ○ nope

15. ✓ Grapes ○ Raisins ○ Neither?

16. What's under your bed? Junk

17. **EVER BEEN HYPNOTIZED?** ○ YES ✓ NO

18. Habit you'd want to break with hypnosis? saying wait all the time

19. Concert you'd like a backstage pass 4? Katy Perry

20. **Celebrity crush u have?** Tom Brady

I wish mermaids were real

NAME Reagan

1. Something make-believe that u wish was real? Unicorns

2. Something real that u wish was make-believe? Snakes

3. Last conversation I had was with __mom__ about __being crabby__.

4. Where do u do most of your heavy thinking? room

5. Wash hair ○ every day ☑ every other day ○ twice a week?

6. ULTIMATE ROAD TRIP GAME? ABC

7. ○ Patient ☑ Impatient?

8. Something u own that would surprise friends? crime book

9. ☑ Early ○ On time ○ Late person?

10. SOMETHING DUMB U DID as a LiTTLE KiD? talked back

11. Ever used a toothpick? ○ yes, don't tell anyone ☑ no way

12. How do u wear your hair most of the time? down

13. Ever gotten into poison ivy? ☑ yes! itchy! ○ no

14. Ever dress up your pet? ○ no pet :(☑ no! ○ yes! With what? _____

15. **Talk during movies?** ○ never ☑ sometimes a little ○ always

16. Sing in the shower? ○ no ☑ yes. How do u sound? OK

17. Scared of clowns? ○ oh yeah ☑ nah

18. ☑ First ☑ Last to raise your hand in class?

19. ☑ Stick to plans ○ Wing it?

20. R u a ☑ good ○ great ○ awful photographer?

Guitar Hero® of course

NAME _____

1. **ULTIMATE** video game? _____

2. Ever been seriously lost? ○ no ✓ ○ yes ↘
   What happened? _____

3. Friend ur similar 2? _____

4. Friend ur the exact opposite of? _____

5. How many pairs of jeans do u own? _____

6. Ever written a poem? ○ **No way** ✓ ○ yes

7. ○✓ Mexican ○ Chinese ○ Pizza?

8. Iron your clothes in the a.m.? ○ of course ○✓ r u kidding?

9. Know anyone u think can read ur mind? ○ **No** ○ yes ↘
   Who? _____

10. ○ **Chocolate mints** ○ **Mint gum** ○ **Hard mint candies?**

11. Your house is on fire!
    ↘ **What 1 item would u save?** _____

12. ○ Black
    ○ Refried beans?

13. ○ Cookies ○ Candy?

14. ○ Secret garden ○ Public park?

15. Own slippers? ○ **No** ○ yes ↘
    What do they look like? _____

16. R u most like ○ SpongeBob ○ Patrick ○ Squidward?

17. Most nutritious food u actually like to eat? _____

18. If u could only wear 1 outfit for 1 year
    ↘ **what would it be?** _____

19. Caught not paying attention in class? ○ no ○ of course!

20. Ever been grounded? ○ no ○ yes. What 4? _____

Star-Struck

Name _____

I would **LUV** to star opposite _____ actor _____ in a movie.

It would be so **Cool** to co-star with _____ actress _____ in a movie.

Fave movie character?

SCARIEST MOVIE MONSTER!

WORST MOVIE U'VE SEEN THIS YEAR?

GRAND

BEST MOVIE U'VE SEEN THIS YEAR?

2 FAVE FLICK?

OK, # 3?

Y is it your Fave?

Hottest actor?

Hottest actress?

Best movie kiss?

Fave way to see a flick?
- big screen TV at home
- stadium seating theater
- small local theater

?

Best seat in the theater?
- up high, in the back
- middle
- front & center

POPCORN
(check all that apply)
S M L plain butter xtra butter

Best theater food?

If u were an actor,
what's the 1st thing u would buy when u made it big?

Where would u live? NYC LA other

Like black & white movies?
- yes no

Ever watch a film w/ subtitles?
- oui no

Watch the Oscars?
- yes no

Best chick flick?
_____

ROCK ★ POP

If I had a band,

Name Reagan

1. **IF YOU HAD A BAND, WHAT WOULD U CALL IT?** Classic 3

2. What's most fun to pop? ○ popcorn ◉ bubble wrap ○ balloons?

3. What's your screensaver? Matty from survivor

4. Jeans with ○ flip-flops ○ flats ○ heels ◉ sneakers?

5. *I luv the sound of* Pop music

6. Do straw slurping sounds bug u? ○ yes ◉ no

7. How 'bout nails on a chalkboard? ◉ yes ○ no

8. Hottest place u've ever been? Hawii

9. Coldest place u've ever been? Ohio

10. Do u have ○ awful ○ OK ◉ great handwriting?

11. **ULTIMATE romantic movie?** Love Actually

12. Who do you usually see movies with? Family

13. ○ Candlelight ◉ Lamplight ○ Flashlight?

14. What do ur sunglasses look like? Super awesome

15. ○ **Country house** ◉ Big city condo

16. Coolest person u know? Kaitlyn Judy

17. Most stylish person u know? Katie Babitsky

18. Funniest person u know? Megan Katitus

19. Most annoying? ◉ bad breath ○ smacking gum ○ talking with mouth full

20. *Something u say ur going 2 do but never do?* Clean my room

I would name it after me.

Name Reagan

1. SOMETHING U'D LUV TO WEAR BUT DON'T HAVE THE NERVE? dress

2. Scared 2 travel over tall bridges? ○ oh yeah ⊘ no way, it's safe

3. Ever had food poisoning? ○ no ⊘ yes. What did u eat? ravioli

4. Had an ant farm? ○ yes ⊘ no ○ just the idea makes me sting!

5. Grown Sea-Monkeys®? ⊘ oh yeah ○ no ○ what r those?

6. Who do u text the most? Megan Kahitus

7. Rescued a wild animal? ⊘ no ○ yes. What kind? _____

8. R u ticklish? ○ YES! AHH! ⊘ not really

9. ○ From scratch ⊘ from a box ○ no mac & cheese?

10. I wish my family had a dog

11. Which is worst? ○ Gnats ○ Flies ⊘ Mosquitoes?

12. Watch TV while u eat dinner? ○ always ⊘ sometimes ○ never

13. *Magazine cover u would like to appear on?* teen

14. ⊘ Fall asleep in ○ Scared to death of the dentist's chair?

15. Take the road ⊘ less travelled ○ everyone else follows?

16. Any nervous habits? ⊘ nope ○ yes. What? _____

17. Can u do a backbend? ○ yep ⊘ no, ow!

18. ULTIMATE sundae ingredients? Whip cream, choc sauce, peanut butter cups

19. *Can u tie a knot in a cherry stem with your tongue?* ⊘ no ○ yep ○ huh?

20. What could u write a book about? my life

my tunes

Name Rezgan

What r your top 3 fave bands?
1. Fith Harmony
2. Twenty-one pilots
3. One Direction

What r your top five fave songs?

My House
Title

_____ is perfect to dance to.

Down town
Title

_____ is great to sing with.

Roar?
Title

_____ has the coolest lyrics.

Black Widow
Title

_____ has awesome music.

Thousand Years
Title

_____ is the best overall song.

What's on ur playlist?
(check all that apply)

- ✓ rock
- pop
- alternative
- country
- dance
- rap/hip hop
- other _____

CONCERT IN A
◐ BIG STADIUM ● COOL DANCE CLUB ● SMALL, INTIMATE CLUB?

SEEN ANYONE IN CONCERT? ● NOPE ✓ YEP. WHO?
Justin Bieber and One Direction

WHO R U DYING TO SEE IN CONCERT?
No one

my tunes

Coolest male singer?

J

Hottest female singer?

Best performer look?

- ( ) JEANS & A T-SHIRT
- ( ) SUPER GLAM
- ( ) ANYTHING + A COWBOY HAT

dance

- ( ) with friends
- ( ) alone in your house?
  (in front of a mirror?)
  - ( ) of course
  - ( ) no way!

Coolest lyrics from a song?

Lyrics

_____

_____

_____

_____

Song Title

OH

LAST ALBUM U BOUGHT?

_____

_____

( ) I don't buy ENTIRE Albums! I NEVER like ALL the songs.

COLOR in the LINes?

Name _____

1. Color in the lines? ◯ no ◯ yes
2. How many pillows do you sleep with?
_____

3. ◯ Team ◯ Individual sports?
4. Can u read music? ◯ yes ◯ no
5. What's worth waking up really early 4?
_____

6. Believe in haunted houses? ◯ yes, scary! ◯ no, it's all a hoax!
7. How about psychics? ◯ yes ◯ no, it's a scam
8. Swim in ◯ a pool (boring?) ◯ a lake (alligators?) ◯ the ocean (sharks?)
9. If u could only have 1 hobby, what would it be? _____
10. Libraries r ◯ so cool ◯ too quiet ◯ OK, I guess
11. IF WE HAD 2 B NAMED AFTER PLANETS, WHICH WOULD U CHOOSE? _____
12. How about a city? _____
13. WHAt ABºUt A CºLºR? _____
14. Chew on ice? ◯ no way, that's bad 4 u ◯ oh yeah
15. Bird ever drop something (u know!) on u? ◯ yes, gross! ◯ nope
16. Eakspa igpa atinla? ◯ WHAT?! ◯ esya, Ia oda
17. ULTIMATE fried food? _____
18. Fave color to write with? ◯ black ◯ blue ◯ other _____
19. Send ◯ really wordy ◯ super short text messages?
20. Ever drunk wheat grass? ◯ no ◯ yes
How was it? _____

HOW BORING!

nice

Name _____

1. Color things the correct colors (GREEN GRASS, BLUE SKY)? ○ yes ○ no, how boring!

2. ○ Cityscape ○ Ocean sunset ○ Mountain view?

3. Won an award? ○ nah ○ yes. What 4? _____

4. ○ Sweet ○ Sour ○ Sweet & Sour?

5. ○ Store-bought ○ Homemade Valentine?

6. Best food when it's cold outside? _____

7. How about when it's hot? _____

8. ○ Big ○ Medium ○ Little dogs?

9. ○ BLUSH ○ BUBBLEGUM ○ HOT ○ NO PINK?

10. Meanest thing a sibling's done 2 u? _____

11. Nicest thing a sibling's done 4 u? _____

12. Sit ○ up front ○ in the middle ○ in the back of class?

13. I could beat _____ in an arm wrestling match.

14. Ridden on a horse? ○ yes ○ no

15. ULTIMATE TV network? _____

16. Keep a diary? ○ no ○ yes

17. Read someone else's diary? ○ no, that's private! ○ yeah, I feel bad.

18. New Year's resolutions? ○ no ○ yes. This year's? _____

19. MET A CELEBRITY? ○ no ○ yes, Who? _____

20. How's your singing? ○ Awful! ○ OK ○ Better than average ○ Awesome!

DESERT ISLAND

YOU ARE stranded on a remote island for 1 year . . .
make wise choices OR if u really want to laugh,
write down the 1st thing that comes to ur mind.

U can have one food item (besides ALL the fish you can catch!)
What would u choose?

Sour Patch Kids

1 BEVERAGE? (Besides fresh H20)

Rootbear

What ONE outfit would U
bring to wear?

Top _Tank top_

Bottom _Shorts_

Shoes _Flip flop_

1 AUTHOR
You get all the books they've ever written.

Dr. Suess

1 MAGAZINE
Don't worry, you'll get one a month!

1 FREEBIE ITEM — IT CAN BE ANYTHING . . .

but ur cell phone, most likely won't have good reception . . .
so think of something else.

I Pod

While struggling to survive, what cool thing could u do for 1 whole year?

do anything I want

BEST THING ABOUT SOLO ISLAND LIVING?

- the beach
- ✦ do WHATEVER I want
- great tan
- lots of "alone" time

ICKIEST THING ABOUT UR SO-CALLED PARADISE?

- ✦ too much alone time
- awful sunburn
- learning to fish
- SAND!! in everything!

U R FINALLY RESCUED!

YAY!

1st person u'd want to see?

Eve

1st thing u'd want to do? ➡ Play

1st thing u'd want to eat? ➡ Moldus

HELP!

Do U stare @ people?

Name Reagan

1. Do U stare @ people? ○ No, how rude! ☑ Depends ○ Of course, I can't help it

2. Something u like. (1ST THING THAT COMES TO MIND): Capybaras

3. Something u dislike. (1ST THING THAT COMES TO MIND): Math

4. **Strawberry** ○ **shortcake** ☑ **milkshake** ○ **jam?**

5. IF U WERE FAMOUS, WHAT WOULD BE UR STAGE NAME? Reagan Miele

6. Do u like hugging? ☑ yes ○ not really, it invades my personal space

7. WHAT SPORT DO U REALLY STINK @? Basket Ball

8. Ever take ballet? ☑ **yes** ○ **no**

9. Watch sports on TV ? ○ **no way** ☑ **yes.** What? Soccer, BB, FB

10. Make any cool sound effects? ☑ **nah** ○ **yes.** What? _____

11. R u good at imitating people? ○ **no** ☑ **sort of** ○ **yes**

12. Name of fave stuffed animal when u were a kid? Bunny

13. FUNNIEST ACTOR? Adam Sandler

14. Stuck a piece of chewed gum somewhere? ☑ **no, yuck!** ○ **yes.** _____

15. **ULTIMATE** CURE 4 hiccups? Swallow water upside down ←where?

16. **What's most important to u?** ☑ **looks** ○ **smarts** ☑ **popularity** ○ **other** 1st and 3rd

17. **Ugliest shoes u've owned?** Crocs

18. Spilled something on urself in public? ○ **no** ☑ **yes.** What? water

19. Spilled something on someone else? ○ **no** ☑ **yes.** What? water

20. Have a crush on someone? ○ **not right now** ☑ **yeah**

Name Reagan

1. PERFORMED IN FRONT OF AN AUDIENCE? ○ NO ✓ YES. WHAT 4? Band

2. ULTIMATE condiment? ✓ Mayo ○ Mustard ○ Ketchup ○ All, mixed together

3. What mall store defines your personality? All star Sports

4. 1 thing u argue about w/ parents? School

5. Fold your underwear? ○ yes ✓ r u joking?

6. ✓ It's hard ○ I don't like ○ I LUV to make new friends?

7. Something ur family does together that u LUV? get icecrcam

8. Something ur family does together that u can't stand?

9. HELD A BABY CHICK? ○ yep ✓ nope

10. Been in a parade? ○ no ✓ yes. What didja do? girl scouts

11. Good @ solving mysteries in movies? ○ no ✓ yes, I should be a detective!

12. R U A FREAKY CHANNEL SURFER? ○ oh yeah ✓ no, that's SO ANNOYING!

13. Most creative thing u've done? made a blanket

14. WOULD U GIVE SOMEONE A PEDICURE? ✓ no, FEET R GROSS! ○ sure.

15. Jealous of a brother/sister? ✓ no ○ yes. Y?

16. Do u brag? ○ no ○ sure ✓ ugh, I think so

17. Speak another language? ○ nope ✓ yes. What? Greek

18. WOULD U RATHER ✓ GLOW IN THE DARK ○ SHIMMER IN THE DAYLIGHT?

19. Left an awful movie? ✓ nah ○ yes. Name?

20. My 1st crush was Mitchell when I was 5 - 6 yrs. old.

1. SKELETONS ○ GIVE ME THE CREEPS! EW! ● R SO COOL!

2. Fave game show? _Win loose or draw_

3. Game show u think u MIGHT do well on? _family game_

4. ○ Strawberries ○ Bananas ● Oranges ○ Apples
   ○ Pears ○ Other _____ ?

   NaME _____

5. Ever picked your own fruit/veggies from a farm?
   ○ NO ● YES. What? _apples_

6. ○ Piano ○ Acoustic guitar ○ Electric guitar
   ○ Saxophone ● Other _trumpet_ ?

7. I ● can't stand being too busy
   ○ LUV having too much going on.

8. Embarrassing celebrity crush u had when you
   were younger? _justin bieber_

9. Ever gone to camp? ○ NO ● YES
   Name of it? _camp christogher_

10. Want to be in politics?
    ○ Yeah, it would B really cool ● R u kidding me?!

11. I stink at anything requiring ○ artistic ● scientific skills.

12. ● Klutzy ○ Perfectly coordinated?

13. ULTIMATE movie soundtrack? _?_

14. Something u bought that u regret? _?_

15. Grossest thing boys do? _?_

16. I escape by ○ listening to music ● watching TV
    ● getting lost in a book ○ taking a nap.

17. SCARED 2 STAY ALONE IN UR HOUSE @ NIGHT? ● ALWAYS ○ SOMETIMES ○ NOPE

18. Celebrity U would love 2 interview? _adam sandler_

19. Nickname? ● NO ○ YES. How'd u get it?
    _____

20. R U named after anyone? ○ NO ● YES. Who? _Randy_

1. Which is scariest? ○ **VAMPIRE** ● **ZOMBIE** ○ WITCH ○ None, they're not real!

2. Last thing u watched on YouTube? *the duck song*

3. Ever been on YouTube? ○ **NO** ● **YES**

4. Wish u had a twin? ○ no way! ● yeah, that would b cool.

5. If ur BFF were a food, what would she/he be?
   Ky-Ky= Cucumber

6. Cops ● make me feel safe ○ kinda scare me.

7. Seen a waterfall? ○ **NO** ● **YES.** Which one(s)?
   niager Falls

8. ● MySpace ○ Facebook ○ other _____?

9. I would LUV to be famous 4 *track*
   ar saccer.

10. If u had wings, where would u fly 2?
    _____ Y? _____

11. If ur personality were a car, what would it be?
    _____

12. READ UR HOROSCOPE? ○ YES, FOR FUN ○ NO, IT'S ALL MADE UP

13. **ULTIMATE adventure w/ a friend?** _____
    _____

14. I mostly like to be around
    ○ funny ○ smart ○ warm-hearted people.

15. Make wishes & throw coins into fountains? ○ **YES** ○ **NAH**

16. I ○ like to please people ○ don't care what others think.

17. Eat sushi? ○ **NO, GROSS!** ○ **YES.** Fave kind? _____
    _____

18. It's cooler to hang out with ○ girls ○ guys.

19. Something u believed as a little kid? _____

20. I think most people think I'm ○ funny ○ snobby ○ friendly ○ weird.

Name _____

style
conscious

I luv to shop for my clothes @
1. _____
2. _____
3. _____

Store u like 2 visit but usually don't buy from?

Last accessory u bought?

Do u own something
you've never worn?
⬤ No ⬤ Yes
What? _____

I

⬤ put a lot of thought
into what I wear.

⬤ throw my clothes on
quickly.

⬤ just like to be
comfortable.

If I could, I would wear _____ every day.

my closet is mostly full of
⬤ jeans ⬤ skirts ⬤ tops ⬤ other _____.

Most comfortable article of clothing I own is my
_____.

What hat would u never, ever wear?

◯ baseball cap ◯ cowboy hat ◯ beret

◯ other _____

◯ I would try any of them. I LUV hats!

What's ur style?

◯ preppy – smart, not opposed to plaid

◯ boho – romantic, billowy, artsy

◯ punk – edgy, crazy, rock 'n' roll

◯ diva – all glam, glitzy, probably like pink

◯ I don't fit into these molds! Then describe your style. ↘

_____

_____

_____

_____

_____

_____

_____

my faves

T-shirt

Dress

Sweater

Shoes

Bag

Earrings

pick me

pick me

pick me

If you were a dog, what kind would u be?

NAME _____

1. If u were a dog, what kind would u be? _____

2. Choose a secret agent name 4 yourself – _____

3. Which is worth it? ◯ mouth on FIRE from hot sauce ◯ ice cream brain freeze ◯ neither!

4. EAt M&M'S ® ◯ 1 @ A tIME ◯ BY tHE HANDFUL?

5. Ever made a snow angel? ◯ YEP ◯ NOPE ◯ WHAT IS THAT?!

6. ULTIMATE part of a cake? ◯ cake ◯ frosting ◯ filling

7. ◯ Dancing ◯ Listening to music?

8. Ever complete a puzzle? ◯ YES ◯ NO, HOW BORING!

9. What sweet food could u never, ever give up? _____

10. I wish I could be paid to _____.

11. HOW MANY TEETH dO U HaVE? _____

12. How many fillings do u have? _____

13. Do toothpaste WºRMS in the sink bug u? ◯ YES! ◯ NO ◯ WHAT?!

14. Ever been sent to the principal's office? ◯ NO ◯ YES, what 4? _____

15. Is it worth being sick to miss school? ◯ YEP ◯ NOPE ◯ SOMETIMES

16. When do u make your bed? ◯ a.m. ◯ when I'm told 2 ◯ uh, never?

17. ◯ Untie ◯ Kick off sneakers?

18. Ever take the blame 4 something someone else did? ◯ YES ◯ NO

19. Ever blamed someone else 4 something u did? ◯ YES :(◯ NO

20. Magical power u wish u had? _____

NAME _____

1. Would u rather be a ◯ cat & wash yourself ◯ dog & get a bath?

2. Something guys **LUV** that u just don't get? _____

3. ULTIMATE **WINTER** Olympic sport? _____

4. ULTIMATE *summer* Olympic sport? _____

5. Ever wear socks with holes in them? ◯ Sure, if they don't show ◯ NO!

6. I would **LUV** to take care of a ◯ baby ◯ puppy ◯ kitten.

7. Star ◯ gazing (as in the sky) ◯ watching (as in Hollywood)?

8. Open your mouth to put on mascara? ◯ YEAH, WEIRD ◯ NO ◯ DON'T WEAR IT

9. What's ur earliest memory? _____

10. Ever fed a goat? ◯ of course ◯ nah ◯ ew, no, don't they eat your clothes?

11. COOlest thing you've ever made by hand? _____

12. Singer whose songs u own the most of? _____

13. Spit out yucky food & ◯ hide in napkin ◯ put back on plate?

14. Afraid of public speaking? ◯ absolutely ◯ kind of ◯ nope

15. ◯ Grapes ◯ Raisins ◯ Neither?

16. What's under your bed? _____

17. **EVER BEEN HYPNOTIZED?** ◯ YES ◯ NO

18. Habit you'd want to break with hypnosis? _____

19. Concert you'd like a backstage pass 4? _____

20. **Celebrity crush u have?** _____

I wish mermaids were real

NAME_____

1. Something make-believe that u wish was real? _____

2. Something real that u wish was make-believe? _____

3. Last conversation I had was with _____ about _____.

4. Where do u do most of your heavy thinking? _____

5. Wash hair ◯ every day ◯ every other day ◯ twice a week?

6. ULTIMATE ROAD TRIP GAME? _____

7. ◯ Patient ◯ Impatient?

8. Something u own that would surprise friends? _____

9. ◯ Early ◯ On time ◯ Late person?

10. SOMETHING DUMB U DID AS A LITTLE KID? _____

11. Ever used a toothpick? ◯ yes, don't tell anyone ◯ no way

12. How do u wear your hair most of the time? _____

13. Ever gotten into poison ivy? ◯ yes! itchy! ◯ no

14. Ever dress up your pet? ◯ no pet :(◯ no! ◯ yes! With what? _____

15. **Talk during movies?** ◯ never ◯ sometimes a little ◯ always

16. Sing in the shower? ◯ no ◯ yes. How do u sound? _____

17. Scared of clowns? ◯ oh yeah ◯ nah

18. ◯ First ◯ Last to raise your hand in class?

19. ◯ Stick to plans ◯ Wing it?

20. R u a ◯ good ◯ great ◯ awful photographer?

Guitar Hero® of course

NAME _Reagan_

1. **ULTIMATE** video game? _justdance_

2. Ever been seriously lost? ○ no ● yes ↘
   What happened? _I wasn't paying_

3. Friend ur similar 2? _Eve_

4. Friend ur the exact opposite of? _____

5. How many pairs of jeans do u own? _____

6. Ever written a poem? ○ *No way* ○ *yes*

7. ○ Mexican ○ Chinese ○ Pizza?

8. Iron your clothes in the a.m.? ○ of course ○ r u kidding?

9. Know anyone u think can read ur mind? ○ *No* ○ *yes* ↘
   Who? _____

10. ○ Chocolate mints ○ Mint gum ○ Hard mint candies?

11. Your house is on fire!
    ↳ *What 1 item would u save?* _____

12. ○ Black
    ○ Refried beans?

13. ○ Cookies ○ Candy?

14. ○ Secret garden ○ Public park?

15. Own slippers? ○ *No* ○ *yes* ↘
    What do they look like? _____

16. R u most like ○ SpongeBob ○ Patrick ○ Squidward?

17. Most nutritious food u actually like to eat? _____

18. If u could only wear 1 outfit for 1 year
    ↳ *what would it be?* _____

19. Caught not paying attention in class? ○ no ○ of course!

20. Ever been grounded? ○ no ○ yes.
    What 4? _____

Star-Struck

Name_____

I would **LUV** to star opposite _____ actor _____ *in a movie.*

It would be so **Cool** to co-star with _____ actress _____ *in a movie.*

Fave movie character? _____

SCARIEST MOVIE MONSTER! _____

WORST MOVIE U'VE SEEN THIS YEAR? _____

BEST MOVIE U'VE SEEN THIS YEAR? _____

Y is it your Fave?

2 FAVE FLICK?

OK, # 3?

GRAND

Hottest actor?

Hottest actress?

Best movie kiss?

Fave way to see a flick?
- ○ big screen TV at home
- ○ stadium seating theater
- ○ small local theater

?

Best seat in the theater?
- ○ up high, in the back
- ○ middle
- ○ front & center

POPCORN
(check all that apply)
○ S ○ M ○ L ○ plain ○ butter ○ xtra butter

Best theater food?

*If u were an actor,
what's the 1st thing u would buy when u made it big?*

Where would u live? ○ NYC ○ LA ○ other

Like black & white **movies?**
○ yes ○ no

Ever watch a film w/ subtitles?
○ oui ○ no

Watch the Oscars?
○ yes ○ no

Best chick flick?
_____

ROCK ★ POP

If I had a band,

Name **Reagan**

1. IF YOU HAD A BAND, WHAT WOULD U CALL IT? _Tiger Stripes_

2. What's most fun to pop? ○ popcorn ● bubble wrap ○ balloons?

3. What's your screensaver? _____

4. Jeans with ○ flip-flops ○ flats ○ heels ● sneakers?

5. _I luv the sound of_ _butterscoch skratking_

6. Do straw slurping sounds bug u? ○ **yes** ● **no**

7. How 'bout nails on a chalkboard? ● **yes** ○ **no**

8. Hottest place u've ever been? _California_

9. Coldest place u've ever been? _Ohio_

10. Do u have ○ awful ● OK ○ great handwriting?

11. ULTIMATE romantic movie? _don't like them_

12. Who do you usually see movies with? _Family_

13. ● Candlelight ○ Lamplight ○ Flashlight?

14. What do ur sunglasses look like? _black_

15. ● **Country house** ○ Big city condo

16. Coolest person u know? _Jack_

17. Most stylish person u know? _Ava_

18. Funniest person u know? _Nora Z._

19. Most annoying? ● bad breath ○ smacking gum ○ talking with mouth full

20. _Something u say ur going 2 do but never do?_ _pickUp socks_

DANCE HIP-HOP

I would name it after me.

Name _Reagan_

1. SOMETHING U'D LUV TO WEAR BUT DON'T HAVE THE NERVE? _dresses in school_

2. Scared 2 travel over tall bridges? ☑ oh yeah ○ no way, it's safe

3. Ever had food poisoning? ○ no ☑ yes. What did u eat? _ravioli_

4. Had an ant farm? ○ yes ☑ no ○ just the idea makes me sting!

5. Grown Sea-Monkeys®? ☑ oh yeah ○ no ○ what r those?

6. Who do u text the most? _Megan Kratitus_

7. Rescued a wild animal? ○ no ☑ yes. What kind? _mouse_

8. R u ticklish? ☑ YES! AHH! ○ not really

9. ○ From scratch ☑ from a box ○ no mac & cheese?

10. I wish my family had a _doey_

11. Which is worst? ○ Gnats ○ Flies ☑ Mosquitoes?

12. Watch TV while u eat dinner? ○ always ○ sometimes ☑ never

13. *Magazine cover u would like to appear on?* _quizlet_

14. ☑ Fall asleep in ○ Scared to death of the dentist's chair?

15. Take the road ○ less travelled ○ everyone else follows?

16. Any nervous habits? ○ nope ☑ yes. What? _knuckle cracking_

17. Can u do a backbend? ☑ yep ○ no, ow!

18. ULTIMATE sundae ingredients? _whip cream, hot fudge, peanut cups_

19. Can u tie a knot in a cherry stem with your tongue? ☑ no ○ yep ○ huh?

20. What could u write a book about? _my reality_

my tunes

Name _____

What r your top 3 fave bands?

1. 1D
2. R5
3.

What r your top five fave songs?

Title _____

_____ is perfect to dance to.

Title _____

_____ is great to sing with.

Title _____

_____ has the coolest lyrics.

Title _____

_____ has awesome music.

Title

The Fox is the best overall song.

What's on ur playlist?
(check all that apply)

- ⬤ rock
- ⬤ pop
- ⬤ alternative
- ⬤ country
- ⬤ dance
- ⬤ rap/hip hop
- ⬤ other _____

CONCERT IN A
⬤ BIG STADIUM   ⬤ COOL DANCE CLUB   ⬤ SMALL, INTIMATE CLUB?

SEEN ANYONE IN CONCERT?   ⬤ NOPE   ⬤ YEP. WHO?

J13

WHO R U DYING TO SEE IN CONCERT?

_____

my tunes

Coolest male singer?

_____

Hottest female singer?

_____

Best performer look?

- ☐ JEANS & A T-SHIRT
- ☐ SUPER GLAM
- ☐ ANYTHING + A COWBOY HAT

dance

- ☐ with friends
- ☐ alone in your house?
  (in front of a mirror?)
  - ☐ of course
  - ☐ no way!

Coolest lyrics from a song?

Lyrics _____

_____

_____

_____

_____

Song Title

OH

LAST ALBUM U BOUGHT?

_____

_____

☐ I don't buy ENTIRE Albums! I NEVER like ALL the songs.

COLOR IN THE LINES?

Name _Reagan_

1. color in the lines? ○ no ● yes

2. How many pillows do you sleep with?
   one

3. ● Team ○ Individual sports?

4. Can u read music? ○ yes ● no

5. What's worth waking up really early 4?
   I Pod Time

6. Believe in haunted houses? ○ yes, scary! ● no, it's all a hoax!

7. How about psychics? ○ yes ● no, it's a scam

8. Swim in ○ a pool (boring?) ● a lake (alligators?) ○ the ocean (sharks?)

9. If u could only have 1 hobby, what would it be? _art_

10. Libraries r ○ so cool ○ too quiet ● OK, I guess

11. IF WE HAD 2 B NAMED AFTER PLANETS, WHICH WOULD U CHOOSE? _Saturn_

12. How about a city? _new yourk_

13. WHAT ABOUT A COLOR? _Violet_

14. Chew on ice? ○ no way, that's bad 4 u ● oh yeah

15. Bird ever drop something (u know!) on u? ○ yes, gross! ● nope

16. Eakspa igpa atinla? ● WHAT?! ○ esya, Ia oda

17. ULTIMATE fried food? _corn dog_

18. Fave color to write with? ● black ○ blue ○ other _____

19. Send ○ really wordy ● super short text messages?

20. Ever drunk wheat grass? ● no ○ yes
    How was it? _____

HOW BORING!

Name Reagan

nice

1. Color things the correct colors (GREEN GRASS, BLUE SKY)? ☑ **yes** ◯ **no,** how boring!

2. ◯ Cityscape ☑ Ocean sunset ◯ Mountain view?

3. Won an award? ◯ **nah** ☑ **yes.** What 4? fastest mile time

4. ◯ Sweet ◯ Sour ☑ Sweet & Sour?

5. ◯ **Store-bought** ☑ **Homemade Valentine?**

6. Best food when it's cold outside? hot chocolate

7. How about when it's hot? ice cream

8. ☑ Big ◯ Medium ◯ Little dogs?

9. ◯ **BLUSH** ◯ **BUBBLEGUM** ☑ **HOT** ◯ **NO PINK?**

10. *Meanest* thing a sibling's done 2 u? Steal all my money

11. *Nicest* thing a sibling's done 4 u? _____

12. Sit ☑ up front ◯ in the middle ◯ in the back of class?

13. **I could beat** Reese **in an arm wrestling match.**

14. Ridden on a horse? ☑ **yes** ◯ **no**

15. **ULTIMATE TV network?** _____

16. Keep a diary? ◯ **no** ☑ **yes**

17. Read someone else's diary? ◯ **no,** that's private! ☑ **yeah,** I feel bad.

18. New Year's resolutions? ☑ **no** ◯ **yes.** This year's? _____

19. **MET A CELEBRITY?** ◯ **no** ☑ **yes,** Who? Undiana d

20. How's your singing? ◯ Awful! ☑ OK ◯ Better than average ◯ Awesome!

DESERT ISLAND

YOU ARE stranded on a remote island for 1 year... make wise choices OR if u really want to laugh, write down the 1st thing that comes to ur mind.

U can have one food item (besides ALL the fish you can catch!) What would u choose?

Cheese burger

1 BEVERAGE? (Besides fresh H2O)

Root beer

What ONE outfit would U bring to wear?

Top Leapord print shirt

Bottom jeans

Shoes tennis shoes

1 AUTHOR
You get all the books they've ever written.

Twilight Author

1 MAGAZINE
Don't worry, you'll get one a month!

American Girl

1 FREEBIE ITEM — IT CAN BE ANYTHING . . .

but ur cell phone, most likely won't have good reception . . .
so think of something else.

Sewing Kit

While struggling to survive, what cool thing could u do for 1 whole year?

Climb mountains

BEST THING ABOUT SOLO ISLAND LIVING?

- the beach
- ✓ do WHATEVER I want
- great tan
- lots of "alone" time

ICKIEST THING ABOUT UR SO-CALLED PARADISE?

- ✓ too much alone time
- awful sunburn
- learning to fish
- SAND!! in everything!

U R FINALLY RESCUED!

YAY!

1st person u'd want to see?

Mom and Dad

1st thing u'd want to do? ➡ Watch TV

1st thing u'd want to eat? ➡ Candy

HELP!

Do U stare @ people?

Name_____

1. Do U stare @ people? ○ No, how rude! ○ Depends ○ Of course, I can't help it

2. Something u like. (1ST THING THAT COMES TO MIND): _____

3. Something u dislike. (1ST THING THAT COMES TO MIND): _____

4. **Strawberry** ○ **shortcake** ○ **milkshake** ○ **jam?**

5. IF U WERE FAMOUS, WHAT WOULD BE UR STAGE NAME? _____

6. Do u like hugging? ○ yes ○ not really, it invades my personal space

7. WHAT SPORT DO U REALLY STINK @?_____

8. Ever take ballet? ○ **yes** ○ **no**

9. Watch sports on TV ? ○ **no way** ○ **yes.** What? _____

10. Make any cool sound effects? ○ **nah** ○ **yes.** What? _____

11. R u good at imitating people? ○ **no** ○ **sort of** ○ **yes**

12. Name of fave stuffed animal when u were a kid? _____

13. FUNNIEST aCTOR? _____

14. Stuck a piece of chewed gum somewhere? ○ **no, yuck!** ○ **yes.** _____
↖where?

15. **ULTIMATE** CURE 4 hiccups? _____

16. **What's most important to u?** ○ **looks** ○ **smarts** ○ **popularity** ○ **other**_____

17. Ugliest shoes u've owned? _____

18. Spilled something on urself in public? ○ **no** ○ **yes.** What? _____

19. Spilled something on someone else? ○ **no** ○ **yes.** What? _____

20. Have a crush on someone? ○ **not right now** ○ **yeah**

What do u think?

Name _____

1. PERFORMED IN FRONT OF AN AUDIENCE? ◯ NO ◯ YES. WHAT 4? _____

2. ULTIMATE condiment? ◯ Mayo ◯ Mustard ◯ Ketchup ◯ All, mixed together

3. What mall store defines your personality? _____

4. 1 thing u argue about w/ parents? _____

5. Fold your underwear? ◯ yes ◯ r u joking?

6. ◯ It's hard ◯ I don't like ◯ I LUV to make new friends?

7. Something ur family does together that u LUV? _____

8. Something ur family does together that u can't stand? _____

9. HELD A BABY CHICK? ◯ yep ◯ nope

10. Been in a parade? ◯ no ◯ yes. What didja do? _____

11. Good @ solving mysteries in movies? ◯ no ◯ yes, I should be a detective!

12. R U A FREAKY CHANNEL SURFER? ◯ oh yeah ◯ no, that's SO ANNOYING!

13. Most creative thing u've done? _____

14. WOULD U GIVE SOMEONE A PEDICURE? ◯ no, FEET R GROSS! ◯ sure.

15. Jealous of a brother/sister? ◯ no ◯ yes. Y? _____

16. Do u brag? ◯ no ◯ sure ◯ ugh, I think so

17. Speak another language? ◯ nope ◯ yes. What? _____

18. WOULD U RATHER ◯ GLOW IN THE DARK ◯ SHIMMER IN THE DAYLIGHT?

19. Left an awful movie? ◯ nah ◯ yes. Name? _____

20. My 1st crush was _____ when I was _____ yrs. old.

1. SKELETONS ◯ GIVE ME THE CREEPS! EW! ◯ R SO COOL!

2. Fave game show? _____

3. Game show u think u MIGHT do well on? _____

4. ◯ Strawberries ◯ Bananas ◯ Oranges ◯ Apples
   ◯ Pears ◯ Other _____ ?

Name _____

5. Ever picked your own fruit/veggies from a farm?
   ◯ NO ◯ YES. What? _____

6. ◯ Piano ◯ Acoustic guitar ◯ Electric guitar
   ◯ Saxophone ◯ Other _____?

7. I ◯ can't stand being too busy
      ◯ LUV having too much going on.

8. Embarrassing celebrity crush u had when you
   were younger? _____

9. Ever gone to camp? ◯ NO ◯ YES
   Name of it? _____

10. Want to be in politics?
    ◯ Yeah, it would B really cool ◯ R u kidding me?!

11. I stink at anything requiring ◯ artistic ◯ scientific skills.

12. ◯ Klutzy ◯ Perfectly coordinated?

13. ULTIMATE movie soundtrack? _____

14. Something u bought that u regret? _____

15. Grossest thing boys do? _____

16. I escape by ◯ listening to music ◯ watching TV
      ◯ getting lost in a book ◯ taking a nap.

17. SCARED 2 STAY ALONE IN UR HOUSE @ NIGHT? ◯ ALWAYS ◯ SOMETIMES ◯ NOPE

18. Celebrity U would love 2 interview? _____

19. Nickname? ◯ NO ◯ YES. How'd u get it?
    _____

20. R U named after anyone? ◯ NO ◯ YES. Who? _____

1. Which is scariest? ◯ *VAMPIRE* ◯ **ZOMBIE** ◯ WITCH ◯ None, they're not real!

2. Last thing u watched on YouTube? _____

3. Ever been on YouTube? ◯ **NO** ◯ **YES**

4. Wish u had a twin? ◯ no way! ◯ yeah, that would b cool.

5. If ur BFF were a food, what would she/he be?

_____

6. Cops ◯ make me feel safe ◯ kinda scare me.

7. Seen a waterfall? ◯ **NO** ◯ **YES.** Which one(s)?

_____

8. ◯ **MySpace** ◯ **Facebook** ◯ **other** _____?

9. I would LUV to be famous 4 _____

_____.

10. If u had wings, where would u fly 2?

_____ Y? _____

11. If ur personality were a car, what would it be?

_____

12. READ UR HOROSCOPE? ◯ YES, FOR FUN ◯ NO, IT'S ALL MADE UP

13. ULTIMATE adventure w/ a friend? _____

_____

14. I mostly like to be around

◯ funny ◯ smart ◯ warm-hearted people.

15. Make wishes & throw coins into fountains? ◯ **YES** ◯ **NAH**

16. I ◯ like to please people ◯ don't care what others think.

17. Eat sushi? ◯ **NO, GROSS!** ◯ **YES.** Fave kind? _____

_____

18. It's cooler to hang out with ◯ girls ◯ guys.

19. Something u believed as a little kid? _____

20. I think most people think I'm ◯ funny ◯ snobby ◯ friendly ◯ weird.

Name _____

style
conscious

I luv to shop for my clothes @
1. _____
2. _____
3. _____

Store u like 2 visit but usually don't buy from?

Last accessory u bought?

Do u own something
you've never worn?
⬭ No ⬭ Yes
What? _____

Ⅱ

⬭ put a lot of thought
into what I wear.

⬭ throw my clothes on
quickly.

⬭ just like to be
comfortable.

If I could, I would wear _____ every day.

my closet is mostly full of
⬭ jeans ⬭ skirts ⬭ tops ⬭ other _____.

Most comfortable article of clothing I own is my
_____.

What hat would u never, ever wear?
○ baseball cap ○ cowboy hat ○ beret
○ other _____
○ I would try any of them. I LUV hats!

What's ur style?

○ preppy – smart, not opposed to plaid

○ boho – romantic, billowy, artsy

○ punk – edgy, crazy, rock 'n' roll

○ diva – all glam, glitzy, probably like pink

○ I don't fit into these molds! Then describe your style. ↘

_____
_____
_____
_____
_____
_____
_____

my faves

T-shirt	Shoes
Dress	Bag
Sweater	Earrings

If you were a dog, what kind would u be?

NAME _____

1. If u were a dog, what kind would u be? _____

2. Choose a secret agent name 4 yourself – _____

3. Which is worth it? ○ mouth on FIRE from hot sauce ○ ice cream brain freeze ○ neither!

4. EAT M&M'S ® ○ 1 @ A time ○ BY the HANDFUL?

5. Ever made a snow angel? ○ YEP ○ NOPE ○ WHAT IS THAT?!

6. ULTIMATE part of a cake? ○ cake ○ frosting ○ filling

7. ○ Dancing ○ Listening to music?

8. Ever complete a puzzle? ○ YES ○ NO, HOW BORING!

9. What sweet food could u never, ever give up? _____

10. I wish I could be paid to _____.

11. HOW MANY TEETH do U HaVE? _____

12. How many fillings do u have? _____

13. Do toothpaste WºRMS in the sink bug u? ○ YES! ○ NO ○ WHAT?!

14. Ever been sent to the principal's office? ○ NO ○ YES, what 4? _____

15. Is it worth being sick to miss school? ○ YEP ○ NOPE ○ SOMETIMES

16. When do u make your bed? ○ a.m. ○ when I'm told 2 ○ uh, never?

17. ○ Untie ○ Kick off sneakers?

18. Ever take the blame 4 something someone else did? ○ YES ○ NO

19. Ever blamed someone else 4 something u did? ○ YES :(○ NO

20. Magical power u wish u had? _____

don't even think about it

NAME _____

1. Would u rather be a ⚪ cat & wash yourself ⚪ dog & get a bath?

2. Something guys **LUU** that u just don't get? _____

3. ULTIMATE **WINTER** Olympic sport? _____

4. ULTIMATE ʃummer Olympic sport? _____

5. Ever wear socks with holes in them? ⚪ Sure, if they don't show ⚪ NO!

6. I would **LUU** to take care of a ⚪ baby ⚪ puppy ⚪ kitten.

7. Star ⚪ gazing (as in the sky) ⚪ watching (as in Hollywood)?

8. Open your mouth to put on mascara? ⚪ YEAH, WEIRD ⚪ NO ⚪ DON'T WEAR IT

9. What's ur earliest memory? _____

10. Ever fed a goat? ⚪ of course ⚪ nah ⚪ ew, no, don't they eat your clothes?

11. COOLEST thing you've ever made by hand? _____

12. Singer whose songs u own the most of? _____

13. Spit out yucky food & ⚪ hide in napkin ⚪ put back on plate?

14. Afraid of public speaking? ⚪ absolutely ⚪ kind of ⚪ nope

15. ⚪ Grapes ⚪ Raisins ⚪ Neither?

16. What's under your bed? _____

17. EVER BEEN HYPNOTIZED? ⚪ YES ⚪ NO

18. Habit you'd want to break with hypnosis? _____

19. Concert you'd like a backstage pass 4? _____

20. **Celebrity crush u have?** _____

CHECK OUT

coke-or-pepsi.com
Take more quizzes.
Shop online
for cool
c-or-p stuff!

coke
OR
pepsi?